BILLY SCHWER

MAN UP

THE WORLD CHAMPION WAY

MENTAL BOXING®

RETHINK PRESS

First published in Great Britain 2018
by Rethink Press (www.rethinkpress.com)

BILLY SCHWER

Joseph

You're the champ!

Let's get it on!

It's show-time

CONTENTS

INTRODUCTION
THE WARM-UP

Hi, my name is Billy Schwer and I'm a recovering boxer.

Now, you may have a preconceived opinion of me: being a professional boxer, having had all those fights; winning all those titles, bashing people up – or getting bashed up more like (my poor nose, I have no idea how many times it's been broken – what a silly place to put a nose!). But that was back in the day, when all I knew was how to box.

Man Up is designed to inspire and empower people to live their lives with passion, power and purpose. In writing this book, I hope that my story, and how my life has turned around, will encourage you to achieve your dreams, fulfil your true potential, live a life you love, and be who you really want to be.

- Would you like to be able to punch above your weight and win more often?
- Would you like to experience more success?
- Would you like to be a lean, mean, success machine?

If I told you that 80% of all fights are won not through physical skill but through brain power, would that surprise you? In our heads, we're all fighting something (love, family, life, work – you name it!), which is why *Man Up* is designed to help you win, and win more often. After all, life's a bit of a battle, and getting to the top on your own is a constant challenge. It's true that without teamwork the dream don't work. Think about this: who's in your corner? Who's got your back? I know what it takes to be a champion – but I also know what it feels like to be a failure, when the proverbial s**t hits the fan. I'm going to tell you more about my story, how events in my life have affected me, and what I learned as a result, but before that, here's a little background on where my journey began.

When I was boxing full time as a professional in the 90s I won the British, Commonwealth, European, and World Championships. But after my boxing career ended in defeat, I struggled with the transition from being a top-class athlete to dealing with life out there in the real world. I felt safer in the boxing ring, but outside of it I made some really bad decisions and, as a result, I went through some tough times. The first two years of my retirement were the worst two years of my life: I suffered from depression and I wrecked my marriage (which ended in divorce). I was also on my way to becoming bankrupt. I eventually lost my home and moved back in with my parents. Everything I'd fought so long and hard for was now gone and I felt like a complete failure. I went from being a world champion to hitting rock bottom. Now I was left with nothing – no future, no money and no idea about who I really was. I'd always been 'Billy the Boxer' and now I was just Billy – who's Billy? I was lost. It was devastating.

While I was going through my crisis, I realised that who I was (or thought I was) and what I was doing just weren't working. I needed to change. I realised my future was my responsibility and I needed to do something about it. I decided to make a comeback, and fight – but this time, the fight was inside my head, which is how I developed my idea of 'Mental Boxing'.

Do you find yourself having a Mental Boxing match with that little voice in your head? Are you in a constant battle, like there's a war going on inside your head? Is the little voice inside your head constantly jabbing at you with

- Can I?
- Can't I?
- Should I?
- Shouldn't I?
- What if?
- What if I don't?
- What if I do?
- Who am I?
- What am I doing?
- Am I doing the right thing?
- Is it really possible?
- Do I fit in?
- Am I going to look stupid?
- Am I going to get this wrong?
- What am I about?
- What's the point?
- What's my point?

If any of this sounds familiar to you, then join the club. These are the questions/concerns/anxieties that can arise for us as we stumble through our middle age, until we reach the point of 'Oh s**t. Now what? My life's not where I want it to be.' It's a rude awakening.

But with many body shots like this coming our way, we can get stuck. We can get trapped inside our own limited conditioning from the past. This book's about you breaking free from the constraints of the past and creating a whole new future for yourself. If you're stuck, unfulfilled, unsatisfied, and simply continue doing what you're doing without making any changes, you'll end up going to your grave without achieving your full potential.

This book will show you how to confront yourself, how to take yourself on so you can live your future life with passion, power and purpose. This means that from now on you'll be sharing your thoughts and feelings with people who perhaps you've been avoiding, or having conversations you don't want to have. You'll have to live in the present, and learn how to deal with the reality of the 'what's so?' in your life. It won't be easy. No matter where you've got to in your life, or what you bring with you into today, there's still more s**t to come. That's life; it can be tough and we struggle with it. There's so much more that we want from life, but we doubt our belief that we can achieve the future that we want for ourselves. The problem is, by the time we get to middle age, one thing we're really clear about is what we *don't* want – e.g. in our business, in our relationships, in our health – but we don't really know what we do want.

Is that the future you want for yourself? Filled with fear, doubt and negativity? Living without any passion or power, and having no purpose? I didn't think so. That's why you've picked up this book, so from now on let's unlock and unleash your future full potential and your means of fulfilling it. Let's get it on, as they say in the fight game.

It was while I was working on myself that I started to learn how to coach, mentor and train others. It was during this time that I realised how much I *love* people, which shocked me, because I'd spent my whole life bashing people up (or getting bashed up). I've been to the very top in what's arguably the toughest, most demanding, and most brutal sport there is: professional boxing. But when I reached the pinnacle of success it wasn't quite what I thought it was going to be like, and it didn't quite work out how I expected it to. Do you ever find that? Life doesn't work out the way you want it to?

Imagine how I felt when I lost my world title in my first defence, after which I crashed and burned. Since then, however, I've been in a conversation with myself and lots of others about how to survive, thrive and create futures that we want to live into: how to live a life by design, a created life with a compelling future, where we get to make a difference. I've studied many books and followed dozens of courses, taken numerous exams to earn my certificates, and I've spent hundreds, if not thousands, of hours in rooms full of people having conversations about what's possible for us as human beings.

I've learned from the suffering that I've been through and the painful times, when I really struggled until I got to the point where I knew that I was the only person responsible for my future. Don't get me wrong – it's taken a while for me to get to where I am now: happy, fulfilled and satisfied with the knowledge that I am the one totally responsible for designing and creating my future (my life) on a daily basis.

Even if you can't relate to me as a boxer, the point is that we're all fighters. We're all fighting something, and most of the time that thing is ourselves. That's the Mental Boxing match we have on a daily basis. With that in mind, maybe now is the right time for you to knock yourself into shape.

Some of what you'll be asked to do will take courage, such as sharing your thoughts and feelings, maybe for the first time, but whatever you do, don't walk away. Turning your back now can only mean failure… With Mental Boxing, it will take courage to man up to that voice in your head, the one that jabs at you with doubts about what people will think of you. Will they think you're mad or weak? If so, who cares? It doesn't matter. This is about giving you the courage to be vulnerable.

Out of vulnerability, strength and power will arise, although it seems counterintuitive. You may believe being vulnerable is a sign of weakness. I too thought this. I'd been trained and conditioned to attack, defend, resist, confront, and fight. I was a fighter who went into the ring prepared to die. For me, to turn that notion on its head and to start to share all my weaknesses and my flaws, to be vulnerable with other people, were immense challenges. It is going through that process that enables me now to explain it with clarity and confidence. As a professional boxer, it was unthinkable to show any weaknesses. Expressing feelings or emotions was seen as a sign of weakness. Despite needing to be 'made of stone' all my life, it's only recently that I've started to undo all that conditioning and allow the real Billy to show through.

That's why I encourage you to do the same as I did and be willing to take a good look at yourself, go to the depths and really push through your boundaries, to discover who you really are and who you want to become. After each round in this book, I will guide you, step by step, on how to challenge yourself before you decide on your next move. Answer the questions in the exercises honestly, and then share the results with two or three people. Don't worry, by Round 5 you'll get the hang of it, but you'll still need to go the distance if you want to win. I want you to get to Round 12, even if that means you have to take a few on the chin and get a few bruises along the way. Stick with it and follow the 3D Success Model over the next three parts of the book:

- Part One: Facing Your Opponents
- Part Two: Fighting Back
- Part Three: Winning

It's really important, especially for us men, to find the courage to step up, to put ourselves at risk, and be prepared to fail. In the face of defeat, all of us must keep marching on because we are warriors. Be determined and keep going, because it's not about how many times you get knocked down, it's about how many times you get up. We're all fighters, we are champions – each and every one of us.

The things you really want for your future life are out there and available to you – keep on pushing.

If all this sounds difficult to achieve, especially if you feel like you are on your own, remember: you've already taken the first step by reading this book. Afterwards, I want to encourage you to become part of the 'Mental Boxing Movement' (details on how to join are at the end of this book), because I don't want you to feel that you are on your own. This will be your opportunity to embrace the community and become part of a movement where we stick together, interact and support one another.

This introduction was the warm-up – now let's face your opponents in Round 1. Let the Mental Boxing match begin.

PART ONE
FACING YOUR OPPONENTS

ROUND 1

KNOWING YOUR OPPONENTS AND WHO'S IN YOUR CORNER

'The starting point of all achievement is desire.'

NAPOLEON HILL

The truth is, most of us men are well-meaning, good-hearted people who want to live a great life, have great relationships, and be fit, well and healthy. The problem is most of us don't know how to achieve all of this. We find it difficult to express ourselves or share our innermost thoughts. Worse still, something stops many of us from sharing with each other and so we remain stuck inside our heads and never do anything about it.

If this describes you, then I want to help you overcome your fear or suspicion about sharing your thoughts with others. Over the last few years, since I became a personal performance coach, I've seen many positive and transformative changes with my clients once they realise it's OK to share themselves, their hopes, fears and challenges, with other men, their partners and close friends.

For example, when I first sit down with a new group, or an individual, because I'm a former world boxing champion, I already have their attention. They listen and they're eager to hear about my career in the ring, and my life after boxing. What they don't expect is that I share my *whole* story with an open heart and talk honestly about my failings, my insecurities, my weaknesses, my flaws. I speak into their hearts and minds. This allows them to 'show up' and to start talking, to share things with the others in the group – possibly things they've kept locked away, sometimes for years. It doesn't matter what they say: I'm not there to judge them. Because I've already shared my story, allowing myself to be vulnerable, I can then be brutally honest with them in return. The result is that through this act of me sharing my life experience, they gain insight into a whole new future they didn't know existed before.

Many of the guys I've worked with have said that these types of conversations have given them a whole new lease of life, that they experienced a whole new energy flow, and that their future began to look different from the default future they were resigned to. It freed them up; they no longer felt stuck and it was up to them, their responsibility, to create the future.

That's what motivated me to write this book: I wanted to give you access to a whole new future you didn't think was possible, or even available. Sometimes you need to fight for what you really want, and I want you to start fighting now.

My whole life has been about trying to prove something: that I wasn't weak and that I was good enough. Fundamentally, even today, I just want to be good enough, accepted, appreciated and loved. To help you begin to take control and rewrite your future, I've developed a visual model that you can refer to from now on to help you identify where you are at any given point. In this part of the book, I'll show you how to deal with what happens when you're in the negative cycle of doubt, distraction and disappointment.

I firmly believe that we all want to feel good, both physically and mentally, that we want to live happy fulfilling lives, and that we want to be healthy. However, it's too easy for us to get stuck in a negative cycle, which prevents us from achieving or even thinking about what it is that we really want.

By the time you finish reading this book, you'll have new tools to help you overcome the negatives and also tools to help you make the most of the positives, guiding you to what you need to do to get you to where you want to be. That could be anything – something big or small.

As we get going, let's be really clear: your future is your responsibility, it's down to you, I can't do it for you. I'm in your corner and I've got your back, but it's down to you to achieve it. It really doesn't matter what it is, the important thing to remember is that whatever you desire, it's your choice. Win or lose, you choose.

The best way to use the 3D model is to treat it like a framework. Put yourself in the model and follow the methods I'll show you over the next eight rounds, where each element is described in more detail. You'll notice that on the right-hand side there's a continuum, so no matter where you are on any given day, you'll immediately know in your own mind if you're winning or losing. What this does is interrupt your current patterns of thinking and behaviour.

You can step back for a moment and acknowledge where you're at in the cycle because you can actually see it. It's much more powerful as a tool than just talking or thinking about it as if it was some kind of theory. The tool acts as a visual aid alongside the theory and/or your discussions with others. It's much harder to bring ideas to life when they are only stored in the mind. Often our desires are left unfulfilled because the conversations we have with ourselves rarely end well.

The purpose of giving you a visual model to refer to is to help you externalise it. Don't just talk to yourself, take a look at where you're at, and then decide where you need to be heading, and what you need to be doing to get to where you want to be.

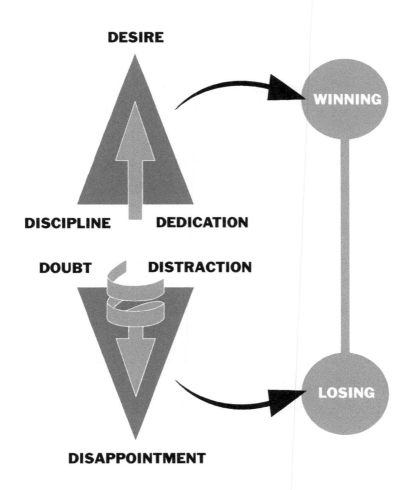

If you see yourself sitting somewhere in the negative cycle, you'll be prompted to try and understand what's happening right now in your life (and why). This interruption offers you the opportunity to shift your focus or direction if you need to.

Don't forget, 'life' happens to us all of the time, both barrels, coming at you full blast, and as a result, it gets in the way, because we have to survive every day. We need to go to work, to provide for our families, pay the bills and put food on the table. Life doesn't always go the way we want and it takes us off track.

That's why I've written this book: to act as an access point to help get men (and women) back into the driving seat of their lives, and to fulfil their desires, because so often we get knocked back, taken off track, and beaten.

Of course, we need to be able to take a few on the chin because the brutal truth is, life doesn't always give us what we want and in order to overcome that, we may have to dig deep. I bet you you've experienced that already, when things just haven't worked out the way you wanted.

So, man up (ladies, too): it's not about how many times you get knocked down, it's about how many times you get up. Accept that you're going to mess things up from time to time, make mistakes; that you're going to fail, or get things wrong. But you have to keep getting up, because that's how champions are made. It's not easy to get up, time and time again, when you've been knocked down – but never, ever give up. Keep using the success model, step up, put yourself at risk and be prepared to overcome each 'failure'. You can see where you are at any given time, so be prepared to step back into the ring: the boxing ring of life.

The negative cycle

Over the next three rounds I'll show you in more detail how to deal with and beat the negative 3Ds: doubt, distraction and disappointment.

Doubt

Self-doubt is like a cancer that nibbles away at you – it's disempowering and makes us totally ineffective. It stops us from having the conversations we probably should be having with the people that are important to us in our lives. Doubt robs us of the courage we need to feel good about ourselves and saps our strength just when we need to be able to go toe to toe with it and fight for what we want. Doubt takes us out of the fight. Ultimately, it stops us from taking action and fulfilling our desires.

Distraction

In the ring, if you get distracted, you're dead. Most people go through life like they're dead, because they're not awake. WAKE UP! You need to wake up, because if you're not pushing, fighting for what you want, seeking, searching, and persistently pursuing your purpose, then you're as good as dead.

Self-doubt can destroy us... or we may even allow the people in our lives, situations or circumstances to kill us off. Rather than finding the courage, and fighting for what we want, we sometimes get distracted, fail, and then blame ourselves or others for not achieving our dreams. The ugly truth is it's too easy to blame other people for our situations or our circumstances, whether it's not feeling good, or not being happy, or not achieving success.

Sometimes our own energy and vibration are off-kilter and this leads to a need for distraction: anything from spending too much time drinking, taking drugs, gambling, having affairs, or doing anything that takes us away from the real world and our own selves, because we can't face being with ourselves.

When things are not how we want them to be, one of the ways we try to deal with this is to focus on what's missing in our lives or what's wrong, but what we really need to do is focus more on what it is we want instead. We need to spend more time and effort visualising our desires and what we really want, and following the next logical step to help us on our way to fulfilling them. Otherwise the impact of distraction can be devastating. We can get lost down the rabbit hole. If that happens, go back to the visual model, take a look and acknowledge where you're at, and get back in touch with the thoughts you have about what it is you want. There's nothing wrong, and the last thing you should do is to beat yourself up if you've been knocked off track. Just stop, refocus, and look at where you're at and where you're going.

Disappointment

Most men I speak to tell me they're not where they thought they were going to be. Deep down, they feel disappointed with themselves and their lives and are left thinking 'Is this it?' Some tell me they feel like they've died and that all their hopes and dreams have died too.

I understand this sense of disappointment, but the only way to deal with this is to be compassionate but also, when they're ready, to be brutally honest and tell it to them like it is: 'This is where you're at in your life, you believe you'll never be truly happy because you're stuck and can't see a way forward, and you spend all your time focusing on the things you *don't* have.'

Men who think like this inevitably end up needing distraction(s). They may turn to drink, drugs, eating – anything to escape. They start to put on weight and live an unhealthy lifestyle, and so begins the downward negative spiral, both mentally and physically. Before they know it, five years have flown by and by now they're in the danger zone, susceptible to strokes and heart attacks brought on by the stress of comparing themselves to other guys who seem, in their eyes, to have it all.

The positive cycle

By the time I get to work with these guys, they've been knocked out by self-doubt, distraction and disappointment.

What I do is give them an access point to very positive outcomes focusing on discipline, dedication and desire. By first facing up to the negatives, they discover they automatically attract the positives and they learn it's not too late to step into the boxing ring of life and fight. They end up saying, 'I can win this; I can be world class.'

I'm not training them to be top-class athletes, but I am showing them how they can perceive themselves as winners. They begin to realise that, although they've been knocked about a bit in the Mental Boxing ring of life, they can still get up, step up, and man up for their future desires. *Man Up* is about being a winner, first in your mind and then out there in the world. The stereotype of the macho man who is afraid to talk and share his feelings and his desires is, as far as I'm concerned, a myth. As soon as men begin to engage in these kinds of conversations, I can see something shifting in them as they realise there are other ways of being and doing.

I'm not suggesting that *every* man who reads this book feels like something inside them has died, or that their life is a complete mess. But my guess is that we all want a little more. Are you willing to take a look at where you're at on the 3D model? If you're not where you want to be, are you willing to put in the work to get there?

No matter who you are, or how successful you are, you still may feel unfulfilled and want more from your life.

So many of us struggle to pick ourselves up off the floor and come back from defeat, setbacks, adversity, depression or possibly debt. No matter what you're fighting, the conversation we're about to have is going to be brutally honest, starting with acknowledging where you're currently at.

What you'll end up understanding are the rules of *Mental Boxing* through the inquiry – experiential learning – that will offer you some insights into your life. While insights are great, it'll be your responsibility to take committed actions as a result. Without that commitment on your part, forget it.

One example of a committed action is to share yourself with others – be that with your business partner, your life partner, or the people you're closest to in your life. This takes courage, but you'll need courage in abundance throughout the book anyway, so be prepared to share your insights with two or three people and tell them what you're up to and are committed to.

Ask for their support in holding you to account to change, shift, and be different, because when you can do that with everybody – round after round in this Mental Boxing match we all fight on a daily basis – then your world will be different from the one it is today.

That's because you'll be showing the world you have integrity by doing what you say you're going to do and doing it when you say you're going to do it. People will respect you more for it, instead of thinking you're the one that never delivers and can't stick to their word. Know that you can, and should, ask for their continued support while you give whatever it is your best shot.

ROUND 2

DOUBT

'When unhappy, one doubts everything;
when happy, one doubts nothing.'

JOSEPH ROUX

DESIRE

DISCIPLINE   DEDICATION

DOUBT   DISTRACTION

DISAPPOINTMENT

Your next move

Life's coming at you from all directions and right now you need to avoid an early exit from the ring. That's why the 3D visual model allows you to look at where you are in the negative or positive cycles and work out what your next move should be – jab and move.

Maybe you've been taking too many on the chin, or you've already been knocked to the canvas. No matter where you are in your life, be that rock bottom or just thinking that there must be more to life, you may be feeling a little unsure of how to make the changes you need to make to get you winning again. Either way, this is the right time to pick yourself up, look at the negative cycle square in the face, and man up to the fact that so far, it maybe getting the better of you. I know how hard that can be and it seems like too high a mountain to climb. That's because as men we're hardwired to believe we can only fight our battles alone.

Even if we do punch above our weight, we may eventually burn out altogether and accept defeat. But it doesn't have to be like that: I'll show you that taking a few steps back from your life and taking a long, hard look at what's really going on isn't a sign of weakness, it's a sign of courage. I know it's not easy to do this on your own, which is why from now on I'll be with you as your personal performance coach. I'll be in your corner; I've got your back, and I'm going to help you win, but you have to play your part. Mental Boxing isn't a quick fix solution and I can't do everything for you, but I'm going to be right there by your side while you're on your way to becoming a champion. From now on, you are literally fighting for your future life, so get ready to summon up your inner warrior spirit.

It's about having humility, compassion and understanding and knowing when to listen to what your team say to you in your corner. You've already got some pretty heavyweight opponents primed to deliver those knockout blows, but with me at your side, in your corner, I'm going to show you how to win. Let's start by weighing in with our first opponent – Doubt.

If you put yourself at risk by entering the ring, the boxing ring of life, you already know you're going to get your ass kicked. As soon as the bell signals the start of the Mental Boxing match, the very idea of stepping into the ring with our first opponent Doubt (or more precisely, Self-doubt), a real heavyweight champion, is enough to make us think twice about showing up in the first place.

Who – or what is – Doubt? When Doubt enters the arena he already knows he's a winner: the name on his back is in big, bold letters, 'The Critic'. As he swaggers into the centre of the ring, the crowd roars its approval and he owns the space around him. He's incredibly athletic, always several steps ahead of us, but he's a dirty fighter who makes up the rules as he goes along. The problem is, he gets away with it, time and time again. One thing's for certain, he's king of the ring. He likes nothing better than to punch below the belt and to keep us on the ropes, relentlessly punching and punching away until we've got nothing left. It's like nobody showed us how to keep our hands up to defend ourselves, or how to jab and move. Instead, we just let him do his worst until that final right hook sends us flying backwards to the floor, landing with an almighty thud. The ref counts down until that's it, another KO win to Doubt. The crowd goes crazy and the medic shines a torch in our eyes to find that everything's gone dull back there. Why is it, then, that we let ourselves get back into the ring with Doubt, aka 'The Critic', over and over again, without any hope of ever defeating him? How can we avoid having (self) doubt in our lives? Is that even possible? The problem is, we all live with self-doubt and the worst critic of all is ourselves.

Self-doubt/self-criticism stops our flow and prevents us from being seen, which ultimately stops us from achieving what we want in our lives in every respect. Self-doubt/self-criticism stems from our past experiences, our thoughts and feelings, and although we may think we've failed as adults, we go right back to childhood to explain this, because a lot of our identity was created in those early days. Where we've failed, where we've made mistakes or haven't seen things through, we created our story around this and formed an opinion of ourselves based on these past experiences.

These experiences are milestones in our past, where Doubt was our opponent and had the upper hand. This, in turn, created a recurring fear that we're going to fail and anxieties about what people think of us or about getting things wrong and looking stupid. This fear is only really triggered by ourselves, fuelled as it is by our self-doubt and expert ability to self-criticise, even without thinking about it. Self-doubt and self-criticism become a learned and automatic response, like learning to drive. After twenty or thirty years we just jump in the car without paying any attention to it. But if we decide to learn and master something new in our lives, sometimes self-doubt can take hold – we become afraid of the risk in case we fail. In turn it numbs us to who we really are. It leaves us feeling mediocre and not reaching the extraordinary potential we all have inside of us. I'm still constantly training myself, listening to others, and educating myself all the time, because I know there's a chance I could easily revert to old habits. Instead, I embrace risk and find the courage to dig deep into myself in order to recreate and reinvent myself as somebody else, rather than relive that past, based on the story of who I was.

The question is: who are you?

It's all too easy to accept being mediocre, because we allow that to be become the norm. If we want to expand beyond that, to confront ourselves and achieve more in life, then it's going to take something more than mediocrity, so we need to face up to the challenges that Doubt presents us with. Doubt is like a hidden boulder in our own river flow; it lurks beneath the surface and gets in the way of our progress – until, that is, we become more self-aware. That's what I'm driving you towards at this stage, to encourage you to become more mindful in your daily routines instead of operating on autopilot, like driving your car and not quite knowing how you really got from A to B. I want you to just pause for a few moments every day and consider that there are other ways of doing things, other ways of being and other ways of communicating.

As things currently sit, we have all failed and life seemingly hasn't gone our way all the time. That's because we allow self-doubt to unconsciously rewire us back to previous occasions when we have failed, and this then becomes a self-fulfilling negative cycle that paralyses us. I can't stress too often that it takes courage to push beyond this, to try things in different ways, even though you've failed or haven't quite got it right, or have said the wrong things, in the past. The one thing you don't want to do is to carry this baggage into your future, because that will only show up as self-doubt and get in your way. Let's not settle for surviving yet another day.

Do you ever feel like you're stuck?

Every day we get up and put on our survival suit and step into the boxing ring of life – the real world – and we survive, albeit dogged by our concerns about looking good and doing the right thing. The last thing we want is people thinking badly of us, or to fail at something, or say the wrong thing. As long as we survive then we feel it's OK, because survival has got us to where we're at right now and tomorrow – guess what? – we'll carry on surviving, running as we do on autopilot as if we're driving our car. But it's time to wake up and understand that those concerns in your life limit your potential, and the possibilities available to you are obstructed from view by what I call 'blind spots'. Self-doubt is a blind spot. If what you really want is to elevate and take yourself to another level, then you have to see Doubt for what it truly is: an obstruction. This is perhaps something you haven't done before because you're too focused on just surviving, even though you're not really fulfilled, happy, or satisfied, without knowing why. The brutal truth is you're stuck.

However, when you understand what, and where, your blind spots are, you can start to address these questions and begin to deal with them. It's going to take courage to face up to what you're dealing with and to those things you begin to notice about yourself. You'll gain an insight that it's self-doubt that stops you having certain conversations with your wife, partner or important people in your life. But once you gain that insight, you can let go of those fears and find the courage to take risks, have those conversations, and ask for support. In so doing, you'll discover that you *are* a worthy opponent of Doubt and that from now on, the crowd might start cheering you on. It doesn't mean that he won't give you hell, but you are now well equipped to defend yourself. The fightback has begun and from now on Doubt might not always be the champion. It's time that 'The Critic' took a few knocks of his own and this will only happen if you have the courage to man up, step up, and be prepared for failure; to put yourself at risk and be ready for the task ahead.

I've talked about Doubt being similar to a boulder in your path, impeding your flow. However, once you begin to negotiate your way around self-doubt, you'll be surprised at how other people find ways of supporting you; more importantly, you'll learn about the people who can't – or won't – support you. Again, one reason we avoid tackling Doubt head on and taking a swing at its dominance in the ring is because we have a fear of being vulnerable, and many of us are not conditioned, or trained enough, for that. Again, events in childhood can be influential in shaping and honing our future self-doubts, especially if we grew up in families where we weren't encouraged to show our emotions or to talk to each other.

Therefore as middle-aged men we may not be used to sitting around a dinner table and talking about our feelings. It's not normal, sharing ourselves, and putting ourselves at risk, because we're afraid of what's going to come back at us. That's why you need to be careful about who you choose to share your thoughts and feelings with. Intuitively, you'll know who the right people to be in your team are, so listen to your gut feeling. Teamwork is essential in enabling you to create your new future and 'without team work, the dream don't work'. With everyone in your team (two or three other people at most) aligned and on course, you'll all be there to support one another. If you're unlucky and share with the wrong people, then what you say to them turns into a version of Chinese whispers and becomes gossip.

So, when choosing your team, you need to act like a gatekeeper of your thoughts and be mindful of who you believe will be right for you. They might not necessarily be part of your own family, because those people might not actually be the right members of your team. The brutal reality is that sometimes the people closest to you aren't always on your wavelength and may not support or empower you when you're looking to make changes. Not everyone likes change. That's because if they see you suddenly going off your normal path a little and making a few mind shifts, it might be uncomfortable for them (maybe more than for you). You can choose not to include those who feel that way. People like that can drag you down, which in turn can present an opportunity for Doubt to land a surprising knockout blow when you're least expecting it.

I'm not suggesting you should be wary of your family. They're still your family and you should treasure that, but you might just have to sack your 'manager' or someone currently on your side if you feel that they can't take your weight on their shoulders from time to time. You want your team to be bullet-proof, staunch, willing to fight alongside you. But make no mistake, this is no easy task, because Doubt dressed up as Fear is a terrifying opponent. I know because I've been trading blows with him since I was a kid. However, you'll be fighting fit before too long and will find yourself landing those knockout blows.

My first experience of overcoming fear was when I was boxing in the National Schoolboy Finals, which was the decider of who was the best in the whole country. Leading up to it, I couldn't eat, I couldn't sleep – I was a complete wreck, absolutely petrified. My dad was my coach, he was the one in my corner (always has been and always will be). When we arrived at the Assembly Rooms in Derby, I remember thinking it was huge and when I walked in, I was terrified. When it came to my turn to box and my dad was putting my gloves on, I said to him:

'Dad, Dad, I can't do it.'

He said, 'What, you can't do it? Bejesus, I don't believe it, you can't do it.' (My dad's Irish by the way). He clipped me around the ear and told it to me straight:

'What do you mean you can't do it? You're joking, this is the final!'

I said, 'Dad, Dad, I'm going to be sick.'

He clipped me around the ear again and said, 'Go on then, be sick.' After which I ran off and found somewhere to throw up – uuuurggghhhh!

I wiped the sick from my mouth, put the gloves on and stepped up into the ring, a petrified young man. Three rounds later I stepped out a champion. I had faced up to Doubt head on (despite my fears) and it wasn't 'The Critic' who won that day. It was in that moment I realised that if I could find the courage to step up, put myself at risk and be prepared to face failure, I could succeed.

We can succeed

That's why I use Mental Boxing throughout this book as a great metaphor for life. By overcoming self-doubt, we can succeed and push through it. As a fighter, you step into the ring and you take a few on the chin. In life outside of the ring, it's just the same; the fight won't always go your way and you'll have to take a few on the chin. Mental Boxing is about manning up and rolling with the punches; it's also about acceptance, being responsible and having integrity. If you know you've given everything you can but don't win, that's nothing to be ashamed of. There's nothing wrong with losing or failing, as long as you have the courage to step back into the ring, the boxing ring of life. Failure is not the final bell; it's about coming back, time and time again. In my case, I failed on my way to the top – and then I had to start all over again.

When I retired from boxing, aged 31, what followed were the worst two years of my life. I'd been world champion and I really doubted I'd be that good at anything ever again. I'd gone from being a top-class athlete to retirement and I just couldn't see a future outside of the boxing ring. I just didn't know what to do with myself. Some days I didn't have the will to get out of bed – I had nothing to get out of bed for, because I had no purpose. My self-doubt questioned whether it really was possible for me to excel at anything else again because I was used to being world class.

My core identity was suddenly missing and this brought about a crisis, leaving me filled with nothing except fear and doubt. The Mental Boxing match I was having at that time was filled with my internal dialogue of 'Can I? Can't I? Shouldn't I? What if?' It was exhausting, draining, and it was constant, that little voice in my head. I really struggled with it. We all know what that's like, constantly having to deal with that little voice in our heads and much of the time it's neither supporting, nor empowering; it's a battle. That little voice is something we all have to listen for and notice. We have to change our focus because we may make mistakes, and often we beat ourselves up for making a 'wrong' move. If we start to let ourselves slip, then we've got to wake up, get things into perspective, and be responsible for preserving ourselves and moving on with integrity.

Otherwise, Doubt is going to kill your passion and power, and rob you of your purpose. If you're passionate, you've got energy, you take inspired actions and you feel powerful as a result.

Don't forget, with Mental Boxing, you're learning how to box clever and be a champion, so never give up. Along the way, you'll suffer some terrible defeats, but you'll also have some great victories, which is why I encourage you to enquire into what's worked for you before and what hasn't. Keep asking yourself, what do you need to look at and what do you need to change to make the difference to allow you to win this championship in this life? An ongoing inquiry in self-learning can help you get around the obstacle of doubt.

Being mindful enables you to see when self-doubt is holding you back, when you're shrinking and playing small. With courage you can step up and put yourself at risk, because that's how champions are made. With every round, when the bell goes, step forward and let your team step backwards out of the ring. But remember they're still behind you, they're in your corner and you can always reach out to them; you are not alone.

These people – your team, the ones you have intuitively chosen to surround yourself with – are on hand to listen, to make eye contact with, to be with, to be empathetic and to offer a smile when it's most needed. Don't ignore them; they are the shoulders on which you will stand tall. After all, they've probably experienced much of what you're going through and they're likely to tell you like it is, to be honest and straight with you. That is who you need on your team, not people who will just agree with you, no matter what you say. You need to be willing to be coachable and take their feedback, which for many of us can initially be difficult to hear, because we're programmed to automatically defend or resist.

Often, our knee-jerk reaction is to attack, defend, resist and confront. Therefore, be mindful of that temptation to attack. In creating your team, you'll need them to help you look at things from a different angle, jab and move, recognise what's not working. That's the part you want to start to dismantle. That reason may initially be hidden from your view but the people in your team can help you uncover it, and then you can have an honest conversation to deal with it. While having self-doubt actually helps us to move forward, a little seed of it can trigger something bigger if left alone. Before we know it, we attract a lot more of it. Then we empower the little seed of doubt and it grows and grows, until it becomes something that gets out of hand. Ignore it and allow it to take control and you run the risk of not being the person you truly are. Win or lose, in Mental Boxing, you choose. My belief is that there is always a reason why we do what we do: the reason why I became a boxer starts a long way back in my childhood.

I was five years of age, in my mum and dad's front room with my two older sisters, Mandy (eleven) and Lisa (eight). We were rolling around on the floor and they were beating me up (again). Just kids being kids, no harm was meant, we were only playing. Mandy was sat upon my chest and Lisa had my arms pinned to the floor. I was kicking and screaming and they were having the time of their lives, waving their long blonde locks in my face while all the time singing Paper Lace's 'Billy, Don't Be A Hero...' I just couldn't fight them off. I got so upset I started to hyperventilate and I turned blue. I thought I was going to die. In that brief moment, I decided that no one would ever beat me up, dominate me, hurt me, or get on top of me ever again.

Also, in that same moment I made a subconscious decision about myself that I was weak because I couldn't fight my sisters off. As a result, I became super tough as a means of covering up and surviving being weak. That ridiculous decision I made about myself as a child became hardwired into my brain, as if it were the truth. There was no way I wanted anyone to know that I was weak. I wanted to hide it, cover it up, and that's how I became 'Billy the Boxer':

from a decision I made at the age of five. That's why I'm still a fighter, even after all these years outside of the ring. How about you – what's your current story? Does it work for you, empower you, get you the life you want, or has it KO'd you?

Ask yourself:
- Do you sometimes feel that you have no choice – that there is no choice?
- Is your life just the way it is – you don't have a say?
- Do you ever wonder how you ended up with the life you have and why you do what you do?
- Have you ever decided something about yourself?
- Is your opinion of yourself empowering you to achieve your dream and get the life you want?

We continuously make decisions about ourselves, and sometimes we may subconsciously choose to be a certain way to cover up and deal with those decisions. As a kid, I decided I was weak, so then I subconsciously chose to become really tough to cover it up, hide it. Being tough became part of my winning formula and boxing was my way of surviving. When I speak at events, I share that story and it helps other people to look at their past and the decisions that they've made about themselves.

Later, when I was 11, I made another decision about myself when I lost my third amateur boxing fight – one I expected to win – to Jason Meager (who's now a good friend of mine). They put Jason's hand up, he beat me, and I was absolutely devastated. I was distraught, crying my eyes out, with my dad consoling me. I remember the decision I made about myself, that I wasn't good enough. I was just a kid, but still, I had programmed my subconscious to convince myself that I was weak and not good enough and I had to overcompensate for it.

How that played out, years later, was that I would go far beyond the normal and train so hard just to prove that I was good enough, that I wasn't weak. That meant training at 5am no matter what the weather could throw at me. In fact, my whole life has been about trying to prove I'm good enough. I've had to confront that as an athlete, as a fighter, and as a man.

I've had to keep going beyond and challenging myself, over and over. Every time I stepped into the ring I had that fear I had as a child of not being good enough. Over time, I learned to deal with that fear, and I learned to step up, confront it, and to challenge it. It was there all the time. It's still there for me now when I speak at an event, and the same emotions and feelings that I used to get when I was going out to fight – the anxiety; the fear of 'Am I going to get it right; will I look good or bad; will people understand my message?' – are still all there. The great thing about being a speaker, though, is that nobody's trying to kill me!

However, while the outcome and intentions are different, the brain still generates the same chemicals and feelings. You might not be a prize fighter but believe me, there's very little difference between boxing in the ring and Mental Boxing out there in the world. All you need to do is summon up the courage to learn from your past stories and to challenge the doubts and the fears that shape your life as it is today.

No matter where you are in your life, address what's working and what's not: do your relationships work? Are you in the right career or right job? No matter what the questions are, you choose – win or lose.

Either you leave it, accept it, or you have a conversation and change things. It boils down to having integrity and being true to yourself, because this affects your behaviours and what you become. None of us are perfect. I believe that the work I've done on myself has allowed me to see myself and my future more clearly. When I retired from boxing, I didn't know who I was. I'd always been 'Billy the Boxer', but who was I as a man? How did I end up the way that I ended up? Why did I go into the ring prepared to die? Where does that killer instinct come from? Do we all possess it, do we all have it?

These questions have been the source of my self-inquiry since I retired from the professional boxing ring, because I needed to unravel and unveil myself to me, just so that I could find and be at peace with myself, to know who I am and then to move forward into the future, free from my past.

My purpose is to inspire and empower people to live their lives with passion, power, and purpose. I'm driven by that, because that's available for us all and that's what I want, for myself and for you. If we don't engage with self-enquiry in this way, we might end up where we don't want to be. When I was going through tough times and was on my way to the bottom, rock bottom, that's when I started to dismantle myself and ask myself 'What's it all about?' Then I really started to pull myself to pieces and look at who Billy was, who I was as a man, and what my future looked like. That's the opportunity I want you to have through reading this book: to have a look at yourself and start the fightback against the things that stop you or keep you stuck. I want to help awaken you to your life purpose.

Through sharing, I'm speaking into your hearts and minds, and I'm reaching into your soul through my own insights. I hope you will discover your own. For now, find the courage to share your self-doubts with three people. Listen to their feedback – and listen to their own sharing, because the more you share with others, the more this will grow. As I stated before, doubt is the killer of passion, power and purpose, but as this round is about to end, you should now know your opponent more fully, so you'll be better trained to throw a few of your own punches next time you meet him in the ring. It's still early days in your fight to be your own champion, and I can tell you that the next opponent waiting to challenge you for your title is as fierce as he is dangerous. Let's get ready to rumble for Round 3 and meet Distraction.

ROUND 3

DISTRACTION

'You can always find a distraction
if you're looking for one.'

TOM KITE

DESIRE

DISCIPLINE   DEDICATION

DOUBT   **DISTRACTION**

DISAPPOINTMENT

Where is your focus?

Are you out of your flow right now? Have you allowed yourself to get distracted – consciously or otherwise – over a period of time but just ignored it, or not even noticed it's happening? Are you really pursuing your desire? Or has someone in your team just told you you're behaving like a right twat and you need to take stock of yourself and your actions? If so, then maybe Distraction has crept up on you and delivered a low blow that you weren't expecting?

Here's the thing: Distraction feeds your ego, but doesn't serve your desire. As a boxer preparing for a fight, there's no way you can allow yourself to be distracted if you want to produce world-class results. When you come up against Distraction in the Mental Boxing ring of life, watch your back. He's a nifty little fella, crafty with it, and doesn't always play by the rules. He'll swiftly move around you, shifting your focus from one point to another in rapid turns so that you start to feel a buzz of excitement as the adrenaline pumps around your veins. After a while, your mind is taken off the fact that this is a fight you're supposed to be winning and it becomes all about you looking good in front of the crowd: unchecked, this will end up as an exhibition match with nothing to show at the end of it.

You'll never leave the ring victorious, but you'll feel on top of the world – yet this is only the precursor until you step into the ring with the deadliest of opponents, Disappointment (which I will discuss in Round 4). All along, you've been taken for a fool and you've been set up by Distraction to fail in the next round.

In your everyday life, it's easy to believe that, on occasions, distraction might be something you need because, let's be honest, it's hard to stay focused and in the zone all of the time. Sometimes, a distraction is welcome, right? However, what I need you to take from Round 3 is that in the world of Mental Boxing you sometimes need to be responsible for how you choose your distractions. Managing that, consciously or subconsciously, is a hard thing to master because, as I know, for a boxer, it's simply not viable to be distracted. Obviously, context is key, and being a boxer is different from life in the real world. But life is what it is – chaotic, unpredictable, reactive, spontaneous – and sometimes we're not aware of being distracted, because of the consequences of the self-doubt that I discussed in Round 2.

That's why, if you take another look at the 3D model at the top of this round, I've shown distraction as part of the negative cycle, and it's in this context that I'm going to discuss it. Distraction is fuelled directly by the result of self-doubt, and it's at that point that you are in danger of being pulled away from attaining your desire in the positive cycle, and so the consequences of our behaviour result in us being firmly sat in disappointment.

Mental Boxing is all about helping you to acknowledge and recognise when you're straying off the path or getting out of your flow. It's so easy for us to get lost and take different pathways because we become distracted. It happens, so when it does – in the same way as dealing with your (self) doubts – you've got to be willing to be open to criticism. Once again, listening to people in your team is vital. We know we don't like to be slammed by other people and that our normal response is to defend, react, resist, confront and challenge whoever is criticising us. We're men – we don't take criticism too well. Distraction can be unproductive, a fruitless pursuit of escapism, where our egos can be let loose because it makes us feel more like men. But the ugly truth is, sooner or later, we have to be aware of the consequences. Again, I'll ask you, where are you at right now? Are you distracted? How do you react to being told you're distracted? Go back and notice where you are in the 3D model *and be honest with yourself.*

Look at the words 'distraction' and 'disappointment' and identify where you're at. It should be immediately clear if you're heading in the wrong direction – the downward spiral – or whether you're heading upwards. Give yourself some credit: you're not stupid, you can tell what's going on within you now that it's been drawn to your attention. You can recognise that distraction is part of the negative cycle, and it's a place where we have trouble accepting that we're lost within our current situation or circumstances. The impact of distraction can be devastating, not just on ourselves, but on all the people around us, at home and at work. We all try to escape reality at some points in our lives – who doesn't? – but sometimes our actions, when we're distracted, are not consistent with our real selves.

As I said at the start of this round, if you lose focus in the boxing ring, you lose sight of what you desire. It's a form of self-imposed brain damage, and it's like throwing in the towel. That's exactly the effect of the downward spiral: it goes on, and on, and on until eventually you end up in the lost years where all your hopes and dreams have faded to nothing.

That part of my life – when I felt lost – is why I wanted to create this concept of Mental Boxing: so that I could help men who have lost their sense of passion, power and purpose. After I retired from boxing, my whole identity seemed to vanish along with my world title. For years, it felt like I was scrambling, trying to find a future, searching for something that I couldn't find. I felt this overwhelming sense of frustration at being unfulfilled; I was unhappy all of the time. I knew I wasn't satisfied with where I was at. It didn't feel good and very quickly I slipped into depression and lost any sense of control. I could see no future for myself outside of the boxing ring and I fell into an abyss of darkness. Sometimes I just had no energy and couldn't find the will to get out of bed. I struggled with trying to do the smallest things in life, and so I sought distractions to fill the void (drugs, sex and rock and roll) – anything that seemed to enable me to escape the reality of my situation. I had no idea how it would affect me and the people around me, but the consequences were devastating. For a start, I wrecked my marriage, which ended in divorce, and then I invested in the wrong people and businesses that didn't work out. Nothing was working out. Eventually, all my mistakes and bad decisions led me to bankruptcy. My home was repossessed, I lost everything, I had no money, I had no future, I hit rock bottom.

It was then that I realised that the way I was being and what I was doing with my life simply weren't working and that I needed to make some changes. That's when I went and got some coaching – a decision that transformed my life and really turned it around. Up until that point, I'd been a world champion and then I'd lost everything and moved back in with my parents (who were absolutely incredible), and I felt like a complete failure.

Does any of my story ring true with you? Are you heading in that downward spiral? Does it seem like your life is getting darker and darker? Do you have less reason to get out of bed in the morning or look after yourself properly? Are you less kind to the people around you? If you feel like this, or if you feel like you're going down these paths, this is a really good time to check yourself and look at the 3D model, and say, 'I'm actually in this zone. I don't want to be where Billy ended up.'

- Ask for help
- Go and share yourself
- Get a coach

If you don't want to reach out to your personal network of people, look outside it. There are plenty of seminars, books to read, and coaches available for you to engage with.

Find the courage to make a change

It's more acceptable now for men to ask for help and the world's a different place since I retired from boxing. As a man, I think we can more readily respect other men's struggles, especially if you've been through some challenges yourself. If you have that level of mindfulness about you, you'll understand that men also respond to compassion, humility, and humanity.

Look at your current reality and ask yourself if it's the one that you want. You might feel like a failure, like I did, but you've got to come back from that. Go toe to toe with your situation as it is now, and allow yourself to actually take it on the chin. Be prepared to take a few more knocks, because no one gets out of the ring unscathed. Don't worry, this is how champions are made. By forgiving yourself you will release resistance, and this will help you get back into your flow. Make amends with those around you that you might have hurt or upset and start to build your bridges.

The important thing is that by recognising your distractions, and being able to step aside from them and acknowledge the impact they have, you will help yourself to move forward. You'll stop being stagnant in that negative cycle, because that's just like death. A lot of the men I work with tell me they feel like they've been dead for some time because they've been stuck in that negative cycle, and that there's nothing left in the future to hope for. Their desires are dead and that's how they see their reality.

Don't get me wrong: I'm not trying to convince you that all the negative elements in your life will suddenly disappear overnight because you've learned to step aside and recognise them. Life is still life; you can't always control it and it comes at you from all directions. To be honest, from time to time, I still fall into that negative cycle. But because I've had lots of coaching and training I'm always in this type of conversation, as it's my business, and now that I've developed my Mental Boxing program, it's much easier to deal with that negative cycle and the distractions, because I have rediscovered my passion, my power and my purpose.

Don't think that this book is a quick-fix solution. Do not believe that after reading it, and applying it, you'll never experience another negative cycle again. What it will do, though, is help you develop strategies to cope as and when you recognise the signs. By the time you've finished the book, you'll know how to deal with them in a better, more positive, productive way. No seminar or book will fix you; you have to fix yourself. I no longer beat myself up if things don't work out the way I wanted them to, or if I make mistakes along the way. The choices that I make are my responsibility, and no one else's. I still have to deal with the consequences, whatever they may be, and be responsible. Things either work out or they don't. The important thing I now know is that I'm not intentionally a bad person. I'm guessing neither are you, so stop beating yourself up because you've let Distraction run rings around you. As I said at the start of the round, Distraction is the warm-up guy for Disappointment and, as we'll find out in Round 4, his sole purpose is to destroy your dreams.

I'm not going to let that happen. One way to beat Disappointment is to start controlling our own narrative, be that in our present or the future. It's so easy to have our narratives written for us, and to be distracted by other people who write what they think our narratives should be. Anything's possible. If I can become a world champion, just a normal kid from Luton who can top the bill in Las Vegas, then anything's possible for you.

ROUND 4

DISAPPOINTMENT

'We must all suffer one of two things: the pain of discipline or the pain of regret or disappointment.'

JIM ROHN

DESIRE

DISCIPLINE   DEDICATION

DOUBT   DISTRACTION

DISAPPOINTMENT

The endgame

When you step into the ring with Disappointment, you need to know that he's the toughest opponent, a ruthless fighter without feelings; he has all the power of Doubt and Distraction behind his killer blows. His one and only objective is to make you end up in one place and one place only – failure.

Doubt, Distraction and Disappointment – together, they are a formidable fighting machine, and without the tools to outbox them that I'm showing you in this book, they'll break you, not make you. Disappointment is the endgame of Doubt and Distraction: you can end up being owned and ruled by it, almost by accident.

If you're being driven by Self-doubt, not fulfilling your hopes, and have been side-lined by Distraction along the way, then Disappointment lies ahead.

I've experienced disappointment many times, especially in the boxing ring. Disappointment hits you hard in the face, because it's about losing, followed by a huge sense of failure. It's lonely in the loser's dressing room. You feel numb all over because a) you've been bashed up and b) you're coming to grips with what's happening in the moment, right now.

That's when you start dealing with the reality of your situation, and it'll take a bit of time to sink in. That's what disappointment does to you, not just in the actual boxing ring but in the Mental Boxing ring of life, but only if you don't know the moves that will help you avoid it. The brutal truth is, if you've already surrendered to your self-doubts and allowed yourself to get distracted, then, ultimately, disappointment will defeat you. That's when you finally crash and burn and hit rock bottom, and that can be a tough place.

The longer you stay there, the more significance you'll attach to Disappointment and you'll end up believing the false evidence that you're a failure. This in turn creates more self-doubt and to counteract that, you end up trying to distract yourself. It's a vicious, downward cycle, which I've shown you in the 3D model. It's all part of the Mental Boxing match that you're having with yourself, which you have little or no hope of winning. That's why I wanted to share with you the tools and resources to mount a challenge – to win and be victorious.

When I found myself staring Disappointment in the face after I lost my world title, I was very fortunate to have some extraordinary people around me, especially my family and close friends, who I always knew were supporting me. Make no mistake, disappointment is a dark place to find yourself in and it's all too easy just to sit there and get stuck. It takes courage and effort to challenge it:

- Are you stuck?
- Are you in a dark place?
- Do you feel like you're a failure?
- Are you stuck in your disappointment?
- Who's really in your corner; is anyone holding you back?

I know it can be tough and a struggle because, as you know by now, I've had my fair share of disappointments, both as a boxer and then, later, as a man. My first disappointment as a professional boxer was when I lost my British and Commonwealth title. Before that, at 23, I was at the top of my game and I'd won the British and Commonwealth titles at the Royal Albert Hall; it was an incredible night, absolutely out of this world. I was unstoppable, until I lost my title in my first defence because of cuts. Back then, disappointment was relatively easy to deal with because, as an athlete at the top of my game, it's like a roller coaster ride anyway: some fights you lose, others you win – back then, losing just fuelled my desire to win next time around. Losing because of cuts didn't make me feel like a failure. It was just a matter of regrouping, and I was lucky because I had a great management team behind me who organised a rematch really quickly – and I regained my title. Throughout my career I felt a burning desire to get to where I wanted to be – world champion – but I knew I had more work to do.

As a British and Commonwealth champion I also rose through the European rankings and I was eventually eligible to challenge for the world title in Las Vegas, the fight capital of the world. But then I got a big cut over each eye and the fight was stopped. Obviously, I was massively disappointed, but in boxing you learn to accept defeat. What I discovered was that I had the ability to fuel my burning desire to become world champion even after my defeats, so disappointment didn't always win. Although I 'failed' in Vegas, I came back again and won the European Championships, which I successfully defended three times until I was able to challenge again for the world title.

This time, I was beaten again on points, yet I felt cheated as my opponent, who had failed a drugs test, won on points but got away with failing the drug test on a technicality. You can imagine my initial huge sense of injustice – but, in boxing, it's like a roller coaster ride: you hit rock bottom but then your desire kicks in and all you want is to win. I was still chasing that world title, so I got back into the driving seat and became really clear on my desire.

My next attempt at the world title went the full twelve rounds and it was a really close fight. I thought I could have won it, but I lost that as well, this time on a split decision. That was three times I hadn't won the world title and once again, I was living with Disappointment. I regrouped with my team and we planned the 'what next?' and still l had the burning desire to become a world champion. On my fourth attempt, I eventually won on points and I fulfilled my burning desire, a lifetime's work in pursuit of a dream.

I was the International Boxing Organisation World Light Welterweight Champion and I'd conquered Disappointment over and over again to get to where I was. Three months later I was back in the ring defending my title, the thing I'd devoted my whole life's dream to winning, only for disaster to strike – I lost. After the fight I woke up in the back of an ambulance on my way to hospital (I'll tell you more about this in Part Two), and that was when I realised my boxing career was over.

It was like the last nail in the coffin, and this is when everything collapsed. Whereas before, when Disappointment had ass-kicked me in the ring, I at least had some hope, because I had the belief in myself that I could try again and keep trying until I fulfilled my desire. Once I'd lost the title and I was in hospital, I knew in my heart that it was all over. That's when Disappointment really got the better of me and showed what a tough opponent he is. My whole future looked blank; I couldn't see a way out of it. It was more final than when I knew I could step back into the ring and try again. Now, I had nothing to fight for. My whole world went dark.

Are you down, but not out?

If you have been knocked down, it's important to keep sight of the fact that it's not about being on the floor, it's about getting up. You may need to recognise that you are repeating negative behaviours. You'll need to approach things from a different angle, because what you're doing is not working. This is how you'll know you need to make some changes. That takes courage and willingness on your part, but manning up and facing it can put you back on the path.

Look at life differently

If you can do that, ultimately, you can change, and you will be able to pick yourself up off the floor. Disappointment, fuelled by your self-doubts and distractions, doesn't need to end up the winner here. You'll also find that the people you've picked to be in your team will start to listen to you differently if you find the power to turn things around, because you're honouring your word.

Sharing yourself with others and being accountable to them for the changes you say you want to make by speaking them into existence, and being consistent with your actions over time – these are the hard bits. If you find the courage to do these things, then you'll be well on the way to knocking Disappointment out of the ring. You won't become a champion overnight. It takes years and years of work and there will be times when you fail or make mistakes, but it's about honouring your words and taking the required actions that are consistent with what you say.

The moment you fail to honour your word and your commitments, you'll start to lose the faith of the people around you. The negative cycle – Doubt, Distraction and Disappointment – will kick in again and you'll never win your Mental Boxing match. As a result, the story you'll keep telling yourself over and over again, to the point that you believe it to be true, is that you're a failure. Like me in my darkest of days, before I turned myself around, you'll eventually just get sick and tired of being sick and tired. You'll fumble your way through and somehow you'll survive, maybe by bluffing your way through it to a certain degree, but then it will all collapse around you again. You'll inevitably end up somewhere down the road in disappointment, and that's when you reach the depths of despair. It doesn't happen overnight, it's a process that breaks down over a period of time. Then you go into denial, thinking: 'It's going to be okay. Things will change. It'll be different.' But in reality, you're in denial because you don't want to – or don't know how to – deal with it.

What I acknowledge now about myself is that I'm fully responsible for everything that I've done: all my successes, all my failings, all my breakdowns, everything – I am 100 percent responsible. Once I realised that, I had the power to find my way through, but it took some time. I needed to unravel and keep reinventing myself until I found me. Part of that process was being willing to forgive myself for all of my mistakes, because forgiving yourself releases resistance. That's why I say to the guys I work with, 'Stop fighting against the "issues" in your life; stop putting up barriers, and just deal with whatever it is you need to deal with.'

Work things through with the right people, and then move on. Just keep moving. No matter how difficult and dark and dangerous it gets for you, there is hope. It sounds like a cliché, but it's true: the only way is up because you can't sink any further. You might be on the floor, but you've actually got to step aside, take a look, refresh, understand, forgive, process and accept that whatever's happened in the past has happened, but that's it, it stays in the past, leave it there. These are not just soft skills, these are tools to actually help you deal with the hard knocks in life and every warrior has these.

Are you a warrior? Have you forgotten or lost sight of these qualities we all have? Because if so, it's not too late. You don't have to let Disappointment get the better of you and lock the door to that dark place from which there is no escaping. You don't need to live your life in daily despair, thinking it would be easier if you just weren't around any more, but knowing you'd never get around to ending it all.

These are the kind of thoughts that ran through my head every day. I just didn't know how to deal with them because there was so much darkness and I wasn't able to focus on the light. But I guarantee that if you keep working on yourself, if you stay open, honest and true to yourself, and remain authentic with the people around you; if you stick to your word and follow through on your intentions, you'll find, over time, that darkness will turn to light. You'll no longer believe the stories that Doubt, Distraction and Disappointment are telling you – that you're a failure, you're not worthy. You'll gain access to another way of thinking and fixing yourself, and you'll be more ready to accept that nothing's a done deal.

Life will change if you know in your heart that there are options, that something else is possible, and that the things you really want, you can achieve. Connecting with your inner self will allow you to access this. Keep telling yourself this, take a moment to look at the 3D model and acknowledge where you are, and Disappointment won't be able to come out on top.

```
┌─────────┐
│  ROUND  │
│    5    │
└─────────┘
```

TAKE STOCK

'Self-reflection entails asking yourself questions about
your values, assessing your strengths and failures,
thinking about your perceptions and interactions
with others, and imagining where you want to
take your life in the future.'

ROBERT L. ROSEN

Reflect

No matter what your life is like right now and no matter where you are with it, you're on the way to winning your championship fight. It's not over yet, you're still going to take a few more blows, but you'll be better equipped to be able to pick yourself up off the floor and try again. Now is a good opportunity to acknowledge what you've been through and inquire into the doubts that you may have about yourself. Step aside from your day for a minute and think about where you might have been distracted or where you've ended up disappointed with yourself. The good news is, the best is yet to come, and even though sometimes it's tough out there, you're in with a better chance of succeeding. Win or lose, you choose.

For me, it was tough outside of the boxing ring. Losing my identity was something I really struggled with, and it took me a while to deal with it. I grappled with it, and went through prolonged periods of self-doubt. I allowed myself to get distracted and, ultimately, I was disappointed, which led to depression, divorce and bankruptcy. I experienced all those things along the way, on my journey to really focusing on what it was that I wanted.

The first few rounds of this book so far have been about helping you to step aside from your life and to recognise the things in your life that might be holding you back. We've faced some fierce opponents who have taken us down paths we never expected or taken us completely off track, sometimes by accident, at other times through choice. Lessons you can take from Part One so far are:

- Don't pay too much attention to Doubt, Distraction, and Disappointment
- Help yourself to get out of the negative and into the positive cycle
- Choose the people in your corner carefully
- Share your thoughts and intentions with clarity and consideration
- Summon up your courage and be willing to make changes
- Focus on your intention and make a commitment

In Part One I've shown you how to make a commitment to shifting the way that you are, especially if you want something else for your life and want to end up in a different place. It's about getting yourself into a positive mindset so that in Part Two, you can fully embrace the positive 3Ds in the visual model to help you move towards what it is that you really want to do with your life. It's about naming and aiming for your desires, which is the starting point of all achievement. Knowing what you want is crucial.

That's why you have to look your first opponent, Doubt, in the Mental Boxing ring (of life) square in the face and go toe to toe, challenging the negativity he attaches to the mistakes that you've made, and the way you feel about yourself. None of it means anything, but Doubt will always play his mind games to make you think differently. Don't let 'The Critic' get the better of you. Stay focused and in your flow, and move on.

It's vital that you see Distraction for what he really is – a highly skilled opponent trained to take your eye off the things that really matter before he lands you with a killer blow, sending you to the floor, where he stamps on your dreams and ambitions of winning.

That's when you destroy Disappointment, the keeper of the dark space, who makes you feel that there is no way out and sends you back into the ring to fight endless rounds with Doubt and Distraction.

Your personal performance coach

In Part Two, allow me to be your personal performance coach. I'm going to guide you to find the access points to getting the best out of your life and creating the world that you want. The great analogy with boxing is that a trainer can see things that you can't see. That's why as an athlete it's an acceptable thing to have a coach, but sometimes in life, we don't feel that we need coaching. My point to you is, we all need life coaching. What a coach sees is something you just can't see – the 'blind spots'. Think of me as your trainer, in the corner looking up at you, but from outside of the ring. I'm looking at life from a completely different place and I see things that you can't. I can see openings and actions that you should be taking that you just can't see because you're in the thick of it. I'm here to guide and support you, which will allow you to then go on to victory. From now on, I'll show you how to craft your future. What that will be is up to you.

In Part Two, we will move into the positive 3D cycle: Discipline, Dedication, and Desire. The next section is about creating a deliberate focus on what your valuable life experiences have taught you. It's a future in which the things you want are what you get. You'll need to be careful about what you focus on by becoming the gatekeeper of your own mind – that's Mental Boxing – which will still challenge you with doubt and distraction. But from now on, you'll know that this is expected and that it's both manageable and OK. The main thing to remember is that wherever you're at now is fine, because the exciting times are ahead of us and the best is yet to come. The future that you're creating is the one you will live into, and now's the time to wake up to that.

In all probability, when you started reading this book you might not have been the type of person who'd ordinarily think about sharing your thoughts or opening up. You might not have really focused on your desires and so felt unfulfilled, and you may have doubted yourself. You'd been open to all sorts of distractions and frequently felt disappointed with various aspects of your life.

Now we've looked in detail at the negative cycles we can all fall into, you'll be able to start thinking about these in a different way. If you've already begun to implement some of the changes I've mentioned so far, you'll have started to notice that people are listening to you more, and they're taking you more seriously. And so are you. In Part Two, you'll begin to see how you can become a creator of your reality. Your world will start to look different because now you are creating it. It's directing your thoughts, and the Mental Boxing match that you have with yourself is about mastering that focus.

We're all fighters – we're all fighting something, right? – and the thing that we're mainly fighting is ourselves. The trick is to decide and focus on what fights you want to win. Don't get caught up in any other dramas that you don't need to get involved in. Be responsible for your own future, because that's what's available. Mental Boxing is the fight each of us has on a daily basis, and we flip-flop from negative to positive cycles. If we're not mindful enough, we can get wiped out in an instant. As we get deeper into Part Two, we'll look at how to jab and move, take it on the chin, roll with the punches, and take inspired actions, because life's always coming at you from different angles. It's not about me motivating you, because I can't do that – it would be like me pushing you up a hill. It's about you getting inspired, and then taking (inspired) de-liberate actions on your path.

We'll keep looking for new approaches and new ways of winning. That way, you'll get to experience yourself differently, because you'll be shifting, growing and developing yourself, and expanding your mind. That's how champions are made.

PART TWO

FIGHTING BACK

ROUND 6

ROLL WITH THE PUNCHES

'Getting knocked down in life
is a given. Getting up and moving
forward is a choice.'

ZIG ZIGLAR

Having discipline and dedication in the unrelenting pursuit of your desire is what will enable you to attain the success you seek. That's what we're aiming for in this segment of the book, where we move on from feeling unfulfilled and, possibly, like a failure, to creating and designing your own future, winning more often, and experiencing more success.

What do you want?

In Part One, Doubt, Distraction and Disappointment had us backed up against the ropes, but now we're in much better shape and ready for the Mental Boxing match ahead. This brings us perfectly into the positive cycle by focusing on the unrelenting pursuit of your desire, starting with discipline, followed by dedication. Moving forward, I'll help you access, through your own efforts, what your desires are and explain how desire itself is the starting point of all achievement. Desire is the first principle of success, but to succeed you have to know what it is you want. Don't be tempted to think it will happen overnight. You're beginning a journey that takes discipline and dedication over time; it's not a quick-fix approach. Instead, this is your opportunity to gain your own insights into particular patterns of behaviour that aren't currently working for you – it's a question of interrupting those patterns, which will then allow you to make changes if needed. The challenge is sticking with that change over time, in order to really embed it and wire it into your brain until it becomes normal behaviour. It's too easy to resist new ways of being and instead allow the constraints of your past to stop your flow. However, if you remain more mindful, then over time you'll be more effective and produce better results, meaning you'll win more often and experience more success in the future you're creating for yourself. You'll learn how to roll with the punches in the Mental Boxing matches you'll be having on a daily basis.

Part Two of this book is, therefore, about learning how to slip, jab and move, and to look at new approaches to win in life – which is still going to come at you from all directions with both barrels, full blast. It's about who you are going to be in the face of everything life is going to throw at you, because you may not have any choice in that. The only choice you must make is how you respond and react to it, and that's what gives you power. Once you have the power and you're in control of yourself, then the pathway through the mess that surrounds you becomes clearer.

That's when you'll experience more success, achieve better results, become more mindful, and be more effective as your life develops around you, with you at its centre.

You've faced and met the opponents, Doubt, Distraction and Disappointment in the ring throughout Part One, so it's time to introduce you to the team members in your corner.

Discipline: it's what got me out of bed at 5am to go running in the rain, sleet and snow, because I was driven by the outcome – to become a champion. It was effort over time and that's the first thing you need to accept – success and winning aren't achieved overnight. I'll be explaining how having self-discipline over time can help you achieve your desire.

Dedication: similar to Discipline, but it's less about the present and is more forward-looking. You need to be dedicated to a future-based, longer-term activity. In my case, that was committing to repeating actions over and over again in my training schedule. For you, dedication to whatever it is you need to repeat again and again is part of the journey to get to the end result, which is Desire.

Desire: this is the fire in your belly. For me as a fighter, it was a burning desire to become world champion and being dedicated to the outcome.

What is the fire in your belly? What do you desire?

Keep telling yourself this: it's having discipline and dedication in the unrelenting pursuit of your desire that will enable you to attain the success you seek. Here's the plan: from now on, I need you to get focused. I want you to be purposeful and to draw a line in the sand, and say to yourself, 'This is it.'

From now on, I want you to set yourself specific tasks and goals, things that you want to achieve for yourself, your business and your life. I'll show you that relentless discipline and dedication in pursuit of your desire will enable you to achieve the goals you're aiming for. Whatever it is you're seeking, it's all about you being completely clear what that is and putting it out there in the world by hammering a stake in the ground and claiming it. In the process, whatever shows up you'll take it on the chin, again and again. In the face of all the 'nos', the upsets, the failures and the setbacks, in the face of getting things wrong, just keep going. When you keep getting knocked down, keep getting up and go again. Don't stop and never give up.

This is your life you're about to start fighting for and you're going to find the courage and the ability to keep marching on. That's what I mean by 'unrelenting'. That's what it's like to be a boxer in the ring.

Take responsibility

In this part of the book, I'm going to help you find the access points to your courage and determination to really achieve what's important for you and for your life. It's time to stop blaming other people for what you're experiencing; it's time to man up and be fully responsible. When you step up into the ring, the boxing ring of life, you are fully responsible; no one is going to save you in there. Be present to it, because from now on it's all down to you. This is your life and your future, which is why you're now facing the positive cycle, moving towards your desire.

It's time for you to step up and I'm going to be your sparring partner. With Discipline, Dedication and Desire in your corner, we're going to learn a lot about each other in the next few chapters. This is the preparation you need for the fight of your life: when I was boxing, sparring was an essential part of my training, development and growth.

I would do over 100 rounds of sparring leading up to a fight. Sparring was really important, because that's where I learned to get the skills that allowed me to go and produce the result in the ring – I was able to fulfil my desire.

It's the same for you – this is the Mental Boxing match you're fighting. With me as your sparring partner, you'll be inquiring into different aspects of your life, which will help you to learn and grow. I'll be there throughout the process to partner and to support you in fulfilling what's important to you and your life.

ROUND 7

DISCIPLINE

'The discipline of desire is the
background of character.'

JOHN LOCKE

DESIRE

DISCIPLINE   **DEDICATION**

DOUBT   **DISTRACTION**

DISAPPOINTMENT

Getting a grip

Boxing is commonly known as the noble art, the sweet science. My philosophy is that by mastering the art and science of Mental Boxing you will unlock and unleash your full potential, so that you're more effective, win more often, and experience more success.

Man has been fighting for millennia. Boxing has evolved, changed and shifted over time, yet some of its historical elements are still alive, such as bare-knuckle boxing.

The sport in which I chose to fulfil my desire has a complex set of rules and laws and I excelled at it: professional boxing. My aim with this book is to help you master the internal mayhem of Mental Boxing because, as a man, if you can get a grip on it, be responsible and self-disciplined, then your life will be different, I guarantee you.

Let me be your personal performance coach and if you're ready to spar with me then the next few rounds will really test you. I'm going to be asking you to man up and face up to your responsibilities, so let's get straight into the ring and begin. Are you ready for this? If not, step aside and go back to the previous rounds and work out what's stopping you: is it Doubt, Distraction or Disappointment? Only when you've figured out how to get back up off the floor to carry on with this Mental Boxing match will you know you're ready. As long as you're prepared to take a few on the chin, I'll show you how to jab and move and avoid the KO blows. You've already come this far, so fight to win.

Discipline (self-discipline) is a vital factor you'll need to master and apply over time to create your future-winning self. Don't even think you can avoid it if you want to succeed and be the best you can be, because it takes effort over time and there are no shortcuts.

Do what you have to do, over and over again, because that's the pathway to success to be the person you want to be. You'll only get there if you harness the power of persistence.

I know that for some guys that can be a struggle – they don't apply self-discipline over time; and then there's a conversation about middle-aged men gaining weight, then losing a little, while all the time feeling they're forever climbing uphill and never reaching the top. Eventually they lose their will to continue, their self-discipline falters and they start slipping backwards. This may or may not describe where you're at on your journey, but whatever area might be slipping away, deep down, you know what you need to do to get things moving forward again.

- What pulls you forward?
- What motivates you every day to take the inspired actions you need to win?
- What's the big 'why' in your life?

Maybe now's the time for you to really connect with why you want to win
Let me help you focus: when you have a burning desire that's strong enough and big enough, as well as a reason why you want to fulfil it, then your self-discipline will automatically kick in and you'll be inspired. If our desires are not strong or burning enough, we tend to fade away. All it takes to start are your thoughts, so when you look in the mirror in the morning, remember, it's about you. Call on your self-discipline, create your day from the get-go, and have a conversation with yourself. That's where it all starts, and your pathway to achieving your desire begins here by you taking control of your thoughts.

Take control of your life

Discipline is about you being proactive – doing it rather than it being done to you. The power lies in the fact that you're actually doing it, and you have the capacity to react and respond to any given changes in circumstances or situations. It's the opposite of when you're in the negative cycle (as in Part One), where the unconscious effects of self-doubt, distraction and disappointment take away your power. However, once you've stepped into the positive cycle you start to make different choices about the direction you're heading in. Win or lose, you get to choose how to create your future day – every day. What you experience in the present moment is the result of the choices and the decisions that you've made in the past. What you'll experience in the future depends on the choices and the decisions that you make today, moment by moment, right now. It's about being self-disciplined.

Being the author of your own life is vital. If you grab this with both hands and on a daily basis create your day with a sense of self-discipline uppermost in your mind, you'll begin to control that Mental Boxing match you'll be having. Creating who you are for yourself in the morning underpins your integrity and that feeds your self-discipline.

You'll begin moving towards your desires and what it is that you really want. You'll also have connected by then with your big 'Why?', because without that nothing is going to happen for you. It will happen, however, if you have the willingness to go beyond and push through your resistance, to go further than you've ever gone before.

As an athlete, I talk about the mind and the body continually working in sync, and both need nutrition as well. You need the fuel to drive your behaviour to carry out both the physical and the mental tasks ahead. Health, fitness and wellbeing are all interconnected and, as a fighter, if you don't put the work in, you don't win. Eighty percent of fights are won in the mind. What connects you and me is that we're all fighting something and seeking out what makes us stand apart from everyone else. In my case, it was ultimately being world champion, but the common thread is the Mental Boxing match that we're all willing to have with ourselves, which, over time, allows us to push beyond our limitations. That's what we're looking to do; to go beyond ourselves knowing that there's no quick fix to any of it. However, once you shift from the negative mindset that we looked at in Part One – once you can manage and be the gatekeeper of your thoughts, when you can break the patterns and habits of your previous thoughts and behaviours – you'll begin to feel the law of attraction working in your favour. Discipline, therefore, is a positive access to your potential desire. Without (self-) discipline, you're screwed: you'll never get to your core. What you desire doesn't need to change the world, just yours.

That's why to win the Mental Boxing match you need to train. I meet so many guys who are desperate to make changes in their lives but don't know where to start because they've never focused on their desires and can't summon up their sense of self-discipline. They're permanently stuck in that negative cycle. For example, sometimes I meet them through a corporate client, such as one who attended my workshops – let's call him 'John' – in his early 40s, clearly stressed, with a busy job that he commuted to, and a young family to provide for.

Over time, he gradually piled on weight, he was out of shape, and this was having a negative effect on his psyche and self-confidence. He didn't want to be that overweight guy sat behind his desk all day with no energy at either end of it. He had lost all his personal motivation, fuelled by his own self-doubts and the anxieties that come with the negative cycle. In a small group, he shared his concerns and feelings aloud for the first time with his peers. What happened afterwards was a mini transformation. The very act of speaking his desire into existence – of wanting to be that leaner, fitter, more determined-to-win guy – ignited his self-discipline to turn his life around through the simple act of running twice a week in his lunch hour. He was supported by a small and trusted team in his corner who encouraged him, listened to him and held him to account. What he discovered in our session together was that he'd lost touch with his integrity, which in his case was related to diet and physical activity.

When you're in unity with your body you'll do what's required, such as eating the right food and maybe not drinking as much. It's not about punishing yourself, but knowing what your desire is and having the willingness to be self-disciplined over time to achieve that. For John, it was a simple objective that required him to take a few small steps. Now, instead of him having that internal conversation with himself – the Mental Boxing match – he's learned how to deal with the negative cycle and move into the positive one, and he is beginning to reap its rewards. By confiding in his team of five others he was able to speak about his desire and then commit to it. However, if John had repeatedly gone back on his word, he would have killed off the willingness of his group to listen to him because they would have thought, 'Oh, he's full of it. He didn't do what he said he would.' Which would have meant that the next time he'd had an idea they'd have shut him down.

Fortunately for John, his simple act of willingly committing to his self-discipline was a success; it not only helped him achieve his desire, it showed his colleagues he was a man of integrity who went way beyond his own personal ambitions. I talked about who you might choose to be in your corner in Part One and how these people might not necessarily be the ones closest to you (as in your immediate family). For John, it worked best for him to have his team made up of people he worked with, because it lent a sense of separation. Also it meant there was little, if no, emotional baggage dragged from his past into his present situation. It allowed space for his desire to breathe without any judgement.

Like our guy John, once you put it out there, your desire becomes more real for you in your head and more real for those who are supporting you, which in turn adds more value to you. You'll discover you can become more effective at work – guaranteed. You'll take better actions, you'll be more conscientious and you'll produce better results.

Hard to believe? Trust me, it works

When I retired from boxing I didn't have the same discipline I had when I was a fighter. In truth, I didn't need it because now my life was totally different. There was no reason for it (in my head) and I no longer had the 'why', so nothing was fuelling any strong enough desire. That's when I looked for something to plough my discipline into because that was missing for me. My context had changed and my identity had vanished. For most people who aren't world class boxers, they go to work, no one's trying to kill them and they survive. Even if they're struggling with whatever they're dealing with, somehow they get through the day. It's all about survival. I just didn't have anything to be disciplined for. What was I surviving for and why? I was drifting around, lost. I kept asking myself, 'What is it that I'm doing? Who are you? What are you? What's the point?' It was only later that I realised that if you're clear about your identity and the outcome that you're trying to achieve, then discipline and dedication (which I'll discuss in the next chapter) will exist naturally because they pull you towards fulfilling your desire. They feed into each another.

These days, I want to wake up in the morning and feel good. Something that gets me into that space is acknowledging all the things I'm grateful for. I might start the day being grateful for three things, such as my health, the people I have in my life, and the future I'm creating. For you, these could be anything you choose. Then, when I get in my car I get really present to the gift of life that I have. It's a deliberate process that I follow and it also takes practice. It's not something that we do automatically. For example, when did you speak out loud your gratitude for the gift of your sight? Or how many times do you give yourself a pat on the back? Is your internal conversation a negative one or do you acknowledge your achievements, no matter how small, to yourself? If you're self-disciplined and you're doing what you need to do, that's all part and parcel of your integrity, and the conversation you'll have with yourself will be empowering and will stem from your self-discipline. This is something you can begin every morning, by deliberately creating your day ahead.

My own personal methods include making time to listen to music that lifts and inspires me, watching an interesting video on YouTube or reading an article online (usually on my phone) so that I start each morning stimulating my mind and soul with all sorts of different messages from areas that I choose to have in my life. This helps me get into a space of appreciation before looking at the actions I'm going to take – or indeed the actions I'm not going to take. As each day begins, I'm consciously creating myself, moment by moment, throughout the day, which informs the things I'll say 'yes' to, as well as those I'll say 'no' to. I find that being able to say 'no' creates a really good space for me. It's me consciously listening to myself and this helps create the structure for my day. It's my deliberate focus, which remains fluid and open to change and, if need be, I will recommit to anything I've not managed to achieve.

What will you say 'yes' or 'no' to today?

Day by day, the more focused you are on where you're putting your energy, the more you'll do and the better the results you'll produce. But remember, if you have one of those days where things haven't gone to plan, it doesn't matter. Life doesn't always do what we want it to; tomorrow will be here soon enough. You might have made a few mistakes or perhaps it just didn't go to plan, but now you can sleep and reset yourself. Tomorrow morning you'll have the opportunity to reinvent and recreate your day.

When you wake up, don't get sucked into the day before; instead, draw a line in the sand, put whatever happened yesterday into the past, because it cannot be undone, and it no longer exists. Then, just be consciously aware of the choices that you're making for the new day ahead and this will drive your communication, your behaviour, and the actions that you need to take. Make sure you structure your day carefully, because it's too easy to end up busy being busy. If you're not clear about what you want to achieve in the day and you're not focused on an outcome, nothing happens. It's this self-discipline that drives and fulfils your intentions.

Discipline is the axis on which this book turns and on which your life will now turn. This is a good time to make an effort to shift your conscious behaviour from the negative to the positive; as a result, you'll begin to make better choices. Take responsibility for your past mistakes and take control of your future actions. If you find yourself fumbling around, struggling, then take some time out, relax, sit down on your own with a coffee and have a little word with yourself, because you are the cause of the noise. Write a list of what you need to do, what actions you need to take, and who you need to call. When you see it on the page it takes the power away from the mental mayhem and you can take back control.

By now you will have worked out that this Mental Boxing match can turn into mayhem if it starts to run away with itself. What you're training yourself to do is master it.

ROUND 8

DEDICATION

'What does it take to be a champion?
Desire, dedication, determination, concentration
and the will to win.'

PATTY BERG

DESIRE

DISCIPLINE   **DEDICATION**

DOUBT   DISTRACTION

DISAPPOINTMENT

Dedication is a process that takes time and is about you committing to your future desire. It doesn't matter what you're dedicating yourself to or whether your desires are big or small. Your desire is whatever you want it to be – just be absolutely clear what that is. Win or lose, you choose.

Are you dedicated enough to commit to, and achieve, your desired outcome?

Now that you're focusing on the positive cycle in more detail, you should be performing and producing better results in the Mental Boxing ring of life. You've learned how to jab and move and to keep your hands up and protect yourself against Doubt, Distraction and Disappointment, but also that when you get knocked down, you have to pick yourself up and carry on with the fight. You've also added Discipline into your training regime and your sparring is becoming more focused, you're producing results now that you're applying these elements to your journey day by day, and now that you have clarity and purpose – you're going somewhere! You're beginning to believe in that lean, mean success machine you've always wanted to be, and when they see that, other people will get excited about it and they will want to come with you on your journey. But there's still more work to do before you can call yourself the champ. The fight's not over yet, and there's still a possibility you can get KO'd in the eleventh or twelfth round – trust me, I've been there.

The difference between now and when you first started reading the book is that the three negative Ds (Doubt, Distraction and Disappointment) were part of your default future that you may have been stuck in. However, now you can see yourself heading towards a strong, positive, compelling, exciting future – a future you're dedicated to. You're attracted to a new energy that you're generating for yourself (no one else will give it to you) and creating a forward momentum, fuelled by your discipline and dedication. This momentum inspires you not only physically and mentally, but also nutritionally as you begin to feel good about yourself.

It's so important for us to pay attention to all these aspects of ourselves, especially our bodies, because our physical being is so connected with our mental being. When we're looking after ourselves physically – be that going to the gym or just going for a walk –we're telling ourselves that we're also on a physical journey. Don't overdo it, don't try to rush it – as I've said, none of this is a quick fix – simply be mindful of taking your time, over time. Learn about your body as you go, from your mistakes as well as from what works. It's about getting the balance right and doing the right kind of exercises, especially for those of us in our middle age, so we can be the best versions of ourselves.

We all make mistakes

Even at this stage it's still possible to mess things up. You might feel like you're behind on points, even though the last few rounds are in your sight. Don't give up: man up and stick with it. None of us are perfect. This book offers an access to a different type of future. If you're willing to do the work and think things through, you can succeed. I can't do the work for you; you have to do it yourself. It doesn't matter where you are right now in your life, it's about you creating and designing a different future. Life's still coming at you from all directions, except you're better prepared to go the distance now that you have the ability to 'jab and move'. If things aren't going your way then perhaps you need to look for a new approach, a new way of winning. You'll still have to take a few on the chin along the way, but now you have more agility and courage, now you can roll with the punches. If you need to, take two steps back to move one forward. This is a twelve-round championship fight and already you've made it to Round

9, but it could still be a close fight. It doesn't matter, though, if you're behind, because you can still win.

Have you got the courage to keep going in the face of adversity?

Things might not be the way that you want them to be and self-doubt might be entering into your mind, but that's what this Mental Boxing match is all about. If Doubt steps back into the ring and tries to outsmart you, interrupt that pattern of thought through Mental Boxing and ask yourself:

- What is it that I want and why do I want it?
- Am I disciplined?
- Am I dedicated?

Acknowledge that you won't – and don't need to – win every round in order to win the title. That's the key – you don't have to win every round to become the champion. If you lose a few rounds and feel a bit bashed up, take time out and regroup and work with your team, the ones in your corner. Don't get sucked into that negative cycle and let Doubt hand over to Distraction and ultimately Disappointment, because any one of those opponents can still kill your dreams.

Instead, allow your team to empower you to focus and get clarity of mind. Be responsible, be that deliberate creator of your reality, and focus on your burning desire. Keep strong, man up. When you step into the centre of the ring and the bell goes, the fight's back on again. You can run but you can't hide. This is life. Face it: you get up in the morning, you go to work, you do your thing and that's it. Better to man up and face it in the ring than give in to denial and delusion. Fight for what you want!

Trust your instinct; you'll know if you're doing the right things and you're on the right path. You can always take advice from your team, the people around you, or your coach. Even if you're moving into new territory, learn from it and listen to your internal guide, which will be telling you how you're feeling about yourself and what you're doing. After all, that little voice in our heads is always there. Try to enjoy the journey (which I know can be difficult at times) and be present to what you're doing, what you have and the people around you. It's so important to live for the moment and yet be committed to the future.

However, don't be attached to the future, be *committed*. When I was boxing, I was so attached to becoming a world champion. Every fight would be three to six months away and after each one I'd start training for the next one. The years rolled by in the process and maybe I could've enjoyed the ride more? What I want you to remember is that you're not in the actual boxing ring, you're in the boxing ring of life. Be present to what you have and what's around you, and enjoy the journey. Be committed to an outcome, but also be committed, not attached, to your desire without losing sight of the present moment.

There's no quick fix

When my boxing career came to an end it took me over ten years to get to where I wanted to be – a fully qualified personal performance coach adding real value to peoples' lives. During that time, I persistently pursued my purpose, and it took years and years and years of dedicated action and training on my part to achieve the outcome I desired. As a result, I'm happier, more fulfilled and more satisfied than I've ever been, because I live in the moment and am present to it, and I get to make a difference.

The great thing about what I'm doing is that there's no final destination. Now I'm a certified Master Practitioner of Neurolinguistic Programming, Timeline Therapy and hypnosis, as well as being a certified personal performance coach. I'm still working on my desire (what it is I want) and I continually dedicate my life to my purpose, part of which is to be able to share my story in such a way that it makes a difference.

That's all happened for me because my self-discipline drove my dedication. That's what's available for you. Now, having gained a few insights about yourself, you're ready to make a few changes or shift your patterns of thinking or behaviour and take committed actions that work towards the outcomes you desire.

Obviously, as a fighter, I was very disciplined and dedicated. I did everything that was required of me to become a world champion. But remember, success didn't happen for me overnight, I had to work at it over time (with discipline and dedication) and I failed three times to win the World Championship. It was on my fourth attempt that I finally achieved the outcome I was working towards. Had I not been dedicated, or if I hadn't had the discipline, there was no way I could have kept going back to the rigours of training and the life I had to lead in order to succeed.

- Are you dedicated to the cause, to the future, the 'something' that you want in life?
- What is it?
- Why do you want it? For what purpose?

If it's still not happening for you, find your courage in the face of defeat to get back up and carry on fighting. Look for new ways of moving forward, which is what I did. Fail your way to the top, wipe away the blood, sweat and tears and get back into the boxing ring of life, because you're only as good as your next fight, the future you're living into. Keep creating it, fight for it.

Leave whatever happened in the past in the past; don't beat yourself up about the mistakes you've made and start reading things into them. You can't undo the past: it is what it is, so learn to live with it, accept it, and don't let it affect your future. The worst thing you can do is to bring your negative past baggage into your future, because it will affect how you respond. You'll be counted out and the fight will be over. React to the moment you are in now.

For example, I've known so many guys who have come out of long-term relationships and have entered new ones with fear and trepidation because they've not learned how to communicate with their partners, how to be truly authentic, or how to man up. They struggle, understandably so, and they have a fear of showing up as their real selves and being vulnerable.

That's usually the result of people being in a marriage for twenty-odd years and thinking they know each other, but in reality they don't any more, because they've drifted apart. It's only when one of them can find the courage to sit down with their partner and start to share themselves authentically that they have the opportunity to reconnect. Of course, that can apply to your partner, spouse, your family members, even your boss. Your past is your past, so don't let it stand in the way of your future.

Man up, show up, communicate – get it dealt with

If something's not working for you, communicating and dealing with the other person is key; don't gossip about it with other people. If you've got an issue with somebody, speak to them directly to find out what's not working for you and try to eradicate the upset that surrounds you. That way you can deal with the negative energy and not carry it into the future, where it will distract you from your discipline, your dedication, and your purpose. It's another skill to master in the boxing ring of life.

At the start of this chapter I asked you to consider whether you were dedicated enough to commit to your desired outcome. I've since taken you on a journey of self-inquiry to help you gain insight into your response by looking more closely at your desire and what that is and, more importantly, why you want it. Your responses are the reason why you will want to be more dedicated, especially if your insights suggest that you're not quite committed enough yet. If the outcomes that you're looking to achieve are strong enough, they're the reason why you should be dedicated, and in the next chapter we'll be looking at the payoffs from your discipline and dedication – your desire. Once you master both discipline and dedication in the positive cycle, you'll begin to build momentum, when all the little wins you achieve along the way count, and also to build your self-belief that you can win big more often and experience more success.

ROUND 9

DESIRE

'I think anything is possible if you have the mindset and the will and desire to do it and put the time in.'

ROGER CLEMENS

DESIRE

DISCIPLINE   **DEDICATION**

DOUBT   **DISTRACTION**

DISAPPOINTMENT

Be unrelenting

I quoted Napoleon Hill, author of *Think and Grow Rich*, at the beginning of this book. He said, 'The starting point of all achievement is desire. The first principle of success is knowing what you want.' This really hits home for me.

Desire is an urge, a thought, and when you speak it into existence and commit to the action required, it takes on a life of its own. It's now out there in the world. Having discipline and dedication in the unrelenting pursuit of your desire is what will enable you to attain the success you seek.

You must be unrelenting, so that you get what it is that you give your attention to, because what you think about you get. Therefore it's important for us to be aware of exactly what it is we're giving our attention to (our future desires) and not to focus on what we think we are lacking or don't have, because that will drive us into the negative cycle (doubt, distraction and disappointment). Since we constantly think about what it is that we want or don't want we need to be the gatekeeper of our minds and our thoughts. As I've said, what you think about is what you get. Keep your attention focused.

We're at the point in the book where you now know how to deal with Doubt, Distraction and Disappointment, and you also now know that these will always be part of your Mental Boxing match. But now the path to achieving your Desire is helped by your Discipline and Dedication over time, both of which are the fuel that will drive your Desire. When you first picked up this book, you might not have known where you were in your life, who was in your team and who would listen to you if you had anything to say. You might not even have been able to articulate what your burning desire might have been. My hope is that as a result of me being in your corner, you've not thrown in the towel in the early rounds, and you are in the fight to win. I've told you I can't fix everything for you, because that's down to you. But what I've given you so far is the access and the tools for you to be able to step back, look at your life, listen to people, share, and then relentlessly pursue your burning desire.

By sharing, you've given language to what might be possible and through your Discipline and Dedication, you've begun to believe and expect that your Desire is achievable – and that feels good. Sometimes we contradict our desires with our beliefs, when subconsciously we may be doubting and not believing it's really possible. That's Mental Boxing. Your unconscious doubt can knock you out, but by being mindful of this you can train yourself to get back into a positive cycle. Then it will become easier, but there will be times when you miss it. Self-doubt will always try to push you back onto the ropes and dominate you, at which point, sit down and take a breather. Tell yourself, 'Okay, let's go again' and you'll start to feel good about yourself and what you're up to. Start looking at things from a different perspective. Jab and move.

It's a bit like a weigh-in before a fight in front of the TV cameras, where the two opponents are sizing each other up and giving each other all the chat. One is Doubt, the other Desire. Make sure you're Desire. By now, you already know Doubt's got some sly tricks up his sleeve to try and knock you out with a surprise left hook, but right now, you can look him in the eye with confidence, because now you've got some moves of your own. You've also got a great team behind you, you're taking good advice, and you're also listening to your own advice. Your disciplined training and dedication to your cause are what will make you a champion; it's Desire who'll be lifting the title belt. Once you've got a strong, burning desire, you're inspired to take the necessary action. Inspiration feels good, inspired action feels even better:

- Do you feel good about what you're doing?
- Are you inspired?

If so, you'll take the necessary inspired actions. Sometimes it sounds like it's hard work; we do it for a short while and then we stop, because we may get knocked out of our flow. By continually taking inspired action and being the deliberate 'author' of your life it will be easier for you to keep going. If you're really connected with the 'why' the 'what' and the 'how' of whatever you're doing, you'll be inspired to take the right actions.

Motivation is different from inspiration: people are motivated to go on a diet or to get fit and they get off to a good start but after a while… I'm sure you know how that story ends for a lot of people. Why does that happen? Because they're not inspired about what they're doing. If you're not inspired, you're going to fail. Be inspired first and let motivation follow.

Be inspired

When I was a boxer I was inspired and I was motivated, but I have to tell you, it was a brutal existence and necessarily so. Life was tough because I was a fighter 24/7. Eat, sleep, live, train and focus on fighting three, five, six months down the road. And that was my life. It was brutal and intense. I've since had time to reflect on what it was that was driving me. I had always been trying to prove something to myself (I still am), that I was good enough and not weak. That's what drove me to pursue my desire to become a champion. I wanted to be different and I wanted to be something special. I didn't get along very well at school: I'm dyslexic and I struggled, and I always say my real education was learned at the University of Hard Knocks, literally, both in the ring and in the boxing ring of life. Boxing was my outlet, and sport was my way to excel at something. When I focused on that, I made it happen through sheer determination. All the while I was managing my disappointments, the upsets, the struggles, the pain and the suffering. I sacrificed a lot of my childhood in pursuit of becoming a champion.

When I was 13 I became the National Schoolboy Champion. From then on I was always in the top five or so boxers in the country, then in Europe and then on a world level. From the age of 13 I'd been used to competing at the top level, but to maintain that and stay there was a challenge. It was through sheer bloody-mindedness and determination, never giving up and pushing through the pain and the suffering, that enabled this. This driving force takes you to places that you don't normally go, especially in a championship fight, when you're in rounds 9 or 10. It's harsh, it's brutal, you're in pain, you're getting battered, pushed to the limit, fighting for your life, but something inside of you keeps going. These days, I find that type of drive and determination to succeed interesting to think about and how that inspired, committed action can be translated in all walks of life. For example, if you suddenly plummet to the depths, it might seem like a dark place, like being in the tenth or eleventh round, still with the possibility you might get knocked out. You may be struggling to stay in the fight, but if you have the belief and the faith in yourself to keep going and to push through, that's when champions are made. If, by these later stages of the fight, you haven't got that faith and belief in yourself, you lose.

The reality is, we are all fighters. What I faced in the ring is exactly the same for all of us outside of it, be that at work, at home, in relationships, in a marriage or a business; it's the same kind of scenario.

Don't give up – fight for what you want

We're in Round 9 now, so if you've done the required action after each round and you've been sharing yourself with others, your training and preparation will be going well. Perhaps your life is already turning out differently because of the changes you've made, and people are also seeing and listening to you differently.

You'll be feeling better about yourself: you might even be eating differently, or have started training – whatever is different, overtly or otherwise, it's part of the ripple effect of being able to manage your thoughts better. Every day, every week and every month, on a cellular level, you're renewing yourself and, over time, transforming yourself. You'll turn yourself into warrior. You'll be more agile, you'll roll with the punches more and you'll be able to jab and move now that you're looking at things differently. You're mentally much stronger.

Nothing in life is a done deal

In Part Three, we'll look at how you need to be more mindful and more self-aware of all the things that will be thrown at you. But as I've said, because you've come this far, you should already notice the differences in how you feel, in how you behave, and especially in how other people respond to you. You're going to be able to face the more challenging things in life with more confidence. You'll be more effective because your experience of yourself and life will be different. You'll be the one creating your thoughts and your future.

In and out of the ring, I've been there and I've done it – which is what makes me different from other performance coaches. When I retired from boxing it took a long time for me to reinvent and recreate a future for myself. I was desperately searching for all the types of futures I thought I could step into.

But I couldn't find anything and that was the biggest challenge I faced. I spent a lot of time, effort and money reinventing myself. I finally reached a point where I awakened to my life purpose, to inspire and empower people to live with passion, power and purpose. However, reaching that point took a long time and for much of it, it was a struggle and a challenge. I didn't know what my future looked like, I didn't have my 'why' or 'what' or how, and I had no idea how to go about finding them. I had become so attached to the outcome of becoming a world boxing champion that that was who I was. When that was gone I went through an identity crisis, because my whole life I'd been 'Billy the Boxer' and now I was just Billy... who's Billy?

The problem was, I didn't really know who Billy was. I knew I needed to find out, though. In the process, I pulled myself to pieces, inquiring into what made me the way I was. It was like I was unravelling and unpacking myself, peeling back the layers. I had to get some freedom from my past – as I mentioned in the previous chapter, the past sometimes constrains us. 'Billy the Boxer' was definitely constraining me and so I had to give up the fight and let him go. That's the point at which I began to reinvent Billy and in truth, I'm still doing that today. The difference is that back then, my whole life as Billy the Boxer was all about me. Now, Billy is not just about Billy, it's more about me being able to work with, support and guide others.

I'm still looking to personally achieve great things in my life. That's why I wrote this book. This book is about you and your life – I'm in your corner and I've got your back. I want you to experience freedom, love, joy, and happiness, and I want you to be fulfilled, happy, and satisfied with life.

That's who I am today – and that, my friend, has me feeling good

I hope you've noticed that my desire is not attached to anything material. The trouble is, we tend to confuse desire with material things: for example, 'I want a new car' (my mate calls those things 'trinkets'), and then when you get the car, it's not enough. I've been through that whole money trap thing and I've lived the high life. But it's not It.

I never imagined I'd say something like this now, but it's true. When I was younger and at the height of my boxing career, I would never have believed anyone if they had told me that I was looking in all the wrong places to feel happy and fulfilled, by filling my life with expensive goods (trinkets). I fell into the same trap a lot of people do – wanting all the nice, expensive things money can buy in the belief that having them will make me feel good.

What does make me feel good is taking the required actions that work towards me achieving and fulfilling my desires. That's when I'm happy and feel good. If the nice cars and houses show up along the way, so be it! Have it all – why not? – it's up to you, but these are no longer the focus of my own desires. It's easy to get attached to such things, but attachment is misery. I know, I've experienced that when winning fight after fight after fight. I just kept moving on to the next one, but now I realise I never really experienced the joy of the moment of what I was doing. I would have brief celebrations, don't get me wrong, but when you spend your whole time looking forward into the future to the next big thing, you lose sight of yourself in the moment. Enjoy the ride, be present.

Of course, your desire is the most important thing to focus on because, as Napoleon Hill says, 'The starting point of all achievement is desire.' In maintaining this focus, it's important to stay present and be present in the moment, to be committed (not attached), and then your desire will happen as you're taking committed actions towards it. Whether it's this week, next week or the month after, keep on keepin' on, keep moving, jabbing and moving.

The main focus in achieving your desire is being happy – now.

PART THREE
WINNING

ROUND 10

PROTECT YOURSELF AT ALL TIMES

'You have power over your mind —
not outside events. Realise this,
and you will find strength.'

MARCUS AURELIUS

Think ahead

Dreams do come true. When I won the world title in front of a capacity crowd at Wembley Conference Centre, it was a lifetime's work in pursuit of a dream. I fulfilled that dream – but then it wasn't quite as sweet as I thought it was going to be because in the twelfth and final round, I got whacked round the back of the head so hard I couldn't see properly.

So, in the last round I had double vision and couldn't see straight; it was like I was hanging on for dear life. I wanted to achieve the dream so badly: this time, I had to win. And I won. It took twenty years of hard graft, discipline and dedication, blood, sweat and tears to win the World Championship belt, and I'd done it.

After I won the fight, everyone on my team and all the supporters backing me were celebrating like crazy, they were euphoric; it was a relief more than anything because this was my fourth attempt at the title. But immediately afterwards, sitting in the changing room, I didn't feel right and I still couldn't see properly: something was wrong. Questions were beginning to form in my head but at that moment, I didn't want to think about them. I wanted to get to the winner's party because I'd done it – I'd achieved my dream and finally I was world champion.

I got myself ready and got in the car with my wife (at the time), who was driving me to the after-fight party back in my home town of Luton, with my parents following on behind. I still didn't feel right. I just didn't feel good. My vision was bad and I started to feel sick. I couldn't hold it any longer; I asked my wife to pull the car over, I jumped out and I was violently sick. Mum and Dad stopped and saw all this happening and the alarm bells started to ring. They took me straight to the Luton and Dunstable hospital, because a friend of mine had been killed in the ring and I also knew guys who'd been brain damaged, and it would sometimes be on their way home that they developed problems.

I was admitted to hospital and it turned out I had concussion, sustained from that whack around the head in the twelfth round. I had had concussion before, but never like that. The upshot was, I missed my own party and stayed under observation for two days with my family around me. I was frightened, I was uncertain of my future health. Of course, when I was discharged, I was still the world champion, and I told myself that everything was OK and I went on holiday.

When I got home, I started to plan my next fight, my first defence. Me being me – greedy, impatient, reckless, mindless – I didn't want to hang around; I had to make having the title pay. Three months later I stepped into the ring again to defend my hard-earned title – and lost. That's when my future took a turn for the worse and I crashed and burned. Looking back now, I returned to the ring too soon after my concussion – even during sparring I got punched in the head and didn't feel right afterwards, and still I ignored the signs. I was committed to keeping the dream alive but wasn't man enough back then to talk to anyone about what was really going on. That way of thinking and behaving is, I now realise, dangerous to us all. I was in denial and I was deluded in the belief that everything would be alright.

I've included this part of my story because none of us can turn back time. One bit of advice I really want you to take away from this book is to try and have some foresight – think ahead, because while hindsight can teach you a thing or two, mostly it does so too late. Recognise what's happening to you in the now and have the courage to speak, and acknowledge, and accept where you're at. It's often said that it's tough at the top, right? I now know it's tougher staying at the top, and because I was so focused on exploiting all that I could from my world title, I ignored what my situation really was and put myself into the 'danger zone' – like a lot of us men do because we're all fighters at heart.

When you're at the 'top' you might get a false sense of security and believe you're invincible. It's easy to convince yourself that you're Superman and that the good times will never end. That's when I found myself in the danger zone and I fully accept responsibility for everything that followed. I was hungry for continued success because I saw myself as a fighter, a winner, a go-getter, unstoppable – that was me. But sometimes that's not who you need to be. I couldn't see past the context of me as a fighter to understand that I really needed to take time off and rest for a little longer instead of being driven to create a financially secure future for myself and my family. I was a fighter.

Three months later, my defence was typical of most of my fights – it was an absolute battle, another war. We knocked each other from pillar to post, round after round after round. It was a brutal. Come the eleventh round, suddenly, that was it, BANG! I got knocked out, game over. I got carried out of the ring on a stretcher and ended up back in hospital, except this time I travelled there in style – in an ambulance. The sirens were blaring and it was dodging through the traffic. I was conscious throughout, but this time I was frightened: I was uncertain about my future health and, more immediately, I didn't want to fall asleep for fear of not waking up. It was in the back of that ambulance that I realised my life as I knew it was over. That was when I made the toughest decision I've ever made – to retire from the professional boxing ring.

Identity crisis

That's also when my whole world fell apart. I went through an identity crisis because for my whole life I'd been Billy the Boxer, and now I was just Billy. Who's Billy? I didn't know anymore.

My questions to you are:
- Have you ever made a life-changing decision?
- Do you ever question who you are and what you're doing?
- Do you ever wonder what's the point, what's it all about?

Tough questions, right?

In my case, I could no longer see a future for myself outside of the boxing ring. I'd been a world champion, so now what? I had no purpose and no vision. I felt empty and alone. I was lost. I really doubted I'd be that good at anything ever again. That's when the negative cycle kicked in and when Doubt showed himself to be a formidable opponent. I really struggled and lost my focus. I took my eye off the ball, dropped my guard, and the impact was devastating. That's when I made some really bad choices and a lot of mistakes. I just couldn't see a way out.

I was depressed, I wrecked my marriage, I suffered a breakdown, and eventually went bankrupt. I lost everything – I was stuck in that negative cycle.

I then went on a journey of self-discovery to find out who Billy was. That took courage, because it wasn't easy to pull myself to pieces, and what I saw wasn't pretty. In all honesty, the first two years of my retirement were the worst years of my life and they seemed to go on forever. I stuck with it, got through the dark times, and came out the other end, because I was willing to go to work on myself. I had to unravel myself and give up my identity. I had to let go of it, and reinvent and recreate, and look for who I now was, and it was only through this process that I realised my life purpose: To inspire and empower people to live their lives with passion, power, and purpose.

That's the part that we sometimes struggle with. We get so attached to our identities, especially if we're athletes – in the same way I was attached to 'Billy the Boxer' – and it's difficult to let go. It's an ongoing process. I'm only just getting the hang of being a man now! Since leaving the world of boxing I've had to man up in different ways, part of which was in facing up to myself as well as the world around me. It's a different type of boxing match now, one that's going on internally, which is why I've written this book. Many of the guys I work with struggle with accepting how their lives need to shift and change so that they can really focus on their desires. They're scared they might not win the fight.

You will, if you keep your hands up and protect yourself at all times, because you may fall into a false sense of security, which is the 'danger zone' that I mentioned earlier. That's when you could get taken out, knocked out like I was in the eleventh round.

Be mindful and consciously aware of yourself and have foresight. Keep creating and generating the future. Keep telling yourself what it is that you want and feeling good about that, and be careful, keep your hands up. Remember, I was close to the end, but I got wiped out.

WE ARE ALL FIGHTERS

'If not you, who?
If not now, when?'

WERNER ERHARD

No matter what you've experienced already – maybe a divorce, separation from your kids, difficult relationships at home or work, or maybe you've experienced financial difficulties – you might have been wiped out already, but I just want to restate that we're all fighters, and I can really appreciate and relate to you because I've been through the same battles as well.

All we can do is learn to deal with ourselves within the situation and the circumstances we find ourselves in. Rather than blame them on everyone else, we can be responsible and, as a result, regain our power. That's when you become a man again instead of being ineffective or mediocre, and you can deal with those situations and the circumstances differently, which is when your life shifts and changes, and this in turn changes the future.

Don't give your power away!

I regained my own power after I attended the Landmark Forum in August 2003, two years after my retirement. I'll never forget it, it rocked my world – I left the building never to be the same again: it was profound. I stood up in front of a room full of 200 or so people and that was my first experience of sharing with others – all 200 of them! I left there feeling lighter, uplifted and empowered, and fully responsible for my future. I discovered that when you share with someone else, it's not only you who feels this way, the other person gets empowered and uplifted also; it's a win-win for everybody.

Looking back, I'm just so, so grateful to have come out of hospital in one piece after my defeat and to have had the opportunity to go and live again. Whereas I needed courage to be a fighter and step into the ring, beat the hell out of somebody and be beaten up, this new way of thinking and looking at myself took a different kind of courage. I'll admit I thought about returning to the boxing ring every week and for a long time, that's all I thought about – how I could make it happen and when. But I knew in my heart of hearts there was no way that I was going be any better than I was in my last fight. I knew, subconsciously, that I'd seen so many fighters make a comeback and so many not do very well in the process and get injured permanently.

Time for a comeback

I knew that as part of my journey I had to give that up and reinvent myself. That's one of the toughest parts an athlete has to deal with – transitioning from one career (and from one life) to another.

A comeback to the ring would have been, for me, a mistake. It was time for me to hang my gloves up and protect myself from myself. That was such a tough decision because I felt I was surrendering, I was entering into the unknown. I was hardwired to be a fighter and that was my identity – 'Billy the Boxer'. When you reach that point, you end up asking yourself, 'Who am I really?', but that's the moment we, as men, need to stop, look and inquire into it, confront it and challenge ourselves. We're so conditioned to think and behave in certain ways that that's who we think we are. Yet it's all fabrication, it's all made up, it's not the truth and this preconceived idea of who we think we are is not who we really are.

- Who are you?
- What do you really want?

More than ever, now is the time you need courage to take a stand for yourself and the future you're creating. Once you start to dismantle how you think and inquire into it, you begin to question the so-called truth of it.

This is one of the calls to action I wanted to feature in this book. I want to encourage you to start questioning that view of the truth, and through your own inquiry-led learning, using the 3D model as an aid, find out exactly who you are.

ROUND 12

WINNING THE TITLE

'History will be kind to me
for I intend to write it.'

WINSTON CHURCHILL

You've reached the twelfth and final round – congratulations! Now you know you can win the Mental Boxing match of life. When you first picked up this book, this might not have been a familiar concept to you but it's one I wanted to introduce to you as a point of access into your own self-inquiry. Mental Boxing is, in fact, very much like life itself – it happens to us every day, all of the time. Much of it is subconscious, but what I hope is that in reading the book, you'll at least give yourself – or will commit to giving yourself – the space and time to take it to front of mind.

I've thought long and hard about Mental Boxing; although I trained as a physical boxer, I've always felt that since I left the ring my skills were transferable into the great lessons of life. There are certain strategies, techniques and ways of thinking that we use in the ring that make boxing the perfect metaphor for people to deal with what life throws at them. As we know, there's a battle out there that challenges and confronts us every day. By using and applying the boxing-winning mindset to the boxing ring of life, you'll keep your hands up and protect yourself at all times. You'll be jabbing and moving more often, looking for new ways of winning; you'll overpower any doubt, distraction and disappointment that might appear, and using discipline, dedication and the team in your corner, you'll achieve your future desires.

- You're a warrior
- You're a winner
- You're a champion
- Keep on fighting for what you want
- Your life depends on it

If you feel like you're falling behind on points in the fight, go back to the 3D model and ask yourself honestly if you've slipped back into the negative cycle. If you have, it doesn't matter, there's no need to beat yourself up, because now you have the tools to make changes. Use the model every day to give you the access from wherever you are to live your life with passion, power and purpose. Your desire is your purpose and that's where your future lies.

Keep going, don't ever give up

From the moment you wake up, deliberately create the day ahead. Even if it doesn't work out the way you want it to, reset and go again tomorrow. Creating your day as a practice helps you to fulfil your daily purpose as it drives you consciously and subconsciously forward.

Keep on moving

Sharing your feelings and thoughts with the other people who you trust in your life, the guys that are in your corner, will help. Sharing isn't a sign of weakness; it's what helps make you a winning warrior. Being vulnerable takes courage and that's what champions are made of.

Having courage will help you create clarity in your life, which will then drive you forward, to make you think about your passion, your power and your purpose. Over time you will begin to focus and deliberately create yourself and the future that you're living into, while being really present and focused in the now moments.

Being present helps you overcome moments of self-doubt and alerts you if you're being distracted. You understand better that disappointment isn't necessarily the end of the road just because you might get knocked down really early or at any point right up to the eleventh or twelfth round in the fight. Now you know you can pick yourself up.

You can still win. It doesn't matter that life may not be going your way at the moment: perhaps right now you might have concerns, for example, wondering if you're in the right job, the right marriage or the right career. You might feel unfulfilled in some way, or you might even be looking for a way out.

You could be acutely aware of your insecurities and weaknesses or you may feel misunderstood. Any one of these, or a combination, might now be urging you to find ways in which you can expand and grow, or wonder how you can become more emotionally intelligent so your relationships at home and at work can be better. Or you may be worried about your health and just want to improve your fitness and wellbeing.

Call to action

No matter what mistakes you've made in your past, remember it's your experiences that teach you. What happened in your past doesn't define you; the past is the past. This is the battle between what's in the past and the default future, knowing that you're going to have to fight your way through, challenge and change it, because if you don't, the result is, you lose.

Instead, step up to the challenge that will shape your future and be prepared to share that with your team, your community and the world if you want; if you need to reinvent yourself in certain areas, go for it. Man up to it and prove to yourself you have real integrity to put yourself out there and create a different future. Never, ever settle for being mediocre because that's the place where a piece of you dies.

There's a reason I've been open and honest in writing this book, because since I retired from the world of boxing I've come to realise that the boxing never really stops and we do battle every day through Mental Boxing. I wanted to share my journey with you, from the highs to the extreme lows; from when I hit rock bottom, to how I got to where I am today. It's not something that happened overnight; it's taken years of self-inquiry and dedicated learning to become trained in the world of self-transformation.

My aim is to create a Mental Boxing community of men where we are able to share our thoughts, concerns, dreams and aspirations freely and without shame or judgement. I recognise there is a huge value to men in being able to have a safe space, and through the work I've done with my clients over the last few years, I know that they find this liberating and empowering. Change is positive, but the fear of stepping into the Mental Boxing ring of life holds too many of us back. I challenge you to step up, put yourself at risk, and go for it, because losing isn't an option. Fight and be the champion you deserve to be.

Come and be part of the Mental Boxing Movement at www.mentalboxing.com and see what lies in store for you there.

ACKNOWLEDGEMENTS

I would like to thank all the men that have passed through my life and taught me many lessons.

I would like to acknowledge all the men that I've battled with, spilled blood with, suffered defeat and victory with in the boxing ring (my brothers).

This is for you.

My dad William Schwer for being by my side, in my corner both inside and outside the ring for my whole life, I owe you dearly.

My mum Wendy for being by his side and mine and taking care of us both.

My sisters Mandy and Lisa for igniting the fight within me, Little Jack for allowing me to relive my youth.

My extended family for the continued love and support that we all receive from one another, that makes life worth living.

Jack Lindsay (Gentleman Jack) my boxing trainer and his wife Ann (I was the third person in their marriage) – I can't express the gratitude and love I have for you both. The sacrifice, time, effort and your expert knowledge that you put into me and my career was truly amazing. You are a true gentleman. Thank you.

To all the men who are in pursuit of a happy life.

This is for you.

Big love to you all.

THE AUTHOR

Billy Schwer is a former British, Commonwealth, European, and World Boxing Champion, and now a personal performance coach. He is also a certified Master Practitioner of Neurolinguistic Programming (NLP), a certified Master Practitioner of Timeline Therapy, a certified Master Practitioner of hypnosis, and a certified Master NLP Coach.

Billy has over ten years' experience in the study of ontology (the study of the art and science of being).

To this Billy can add twenty-three years of boxing experience, which has confirmed to him that 'boxing is a great metaphor for life.' He brings both this experience and his academic studies to his continuing practice and development in the world of personal growth and change.

You can contact Billy at: www.mentalboxing.com

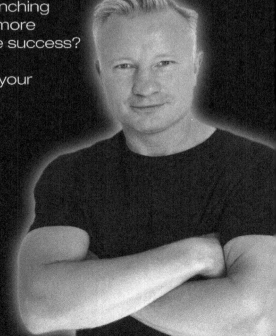